SECOND EDITION

Differentiated Instructional Strategies

for Writing
in the Content Areas

SECOND EDITION

Differentiated
Instructional
Strategies

for Writing
in the Content Areas

Carolyn Chapman · Rita King

CORWIN
A SAGE Company

For information:

Corwin
A SAGE Company
2455 Teller Road
Thousand Oaks, California 91320
(800) 233-9936
Fax: (800) 417-2466
www.corwinpress.com

SAGE Ltd.
1 Oliver's Yard
55 City Road
London EC1Y 1SP
United Kingdom

SAGE India Pvt. Ltd.
B 1/I 1 Mohan Cooperative
    Industrial Area
Mathura Road, New Delhi 110 044
India

SAGE Asia-Pacific Pte. Ltd.
33 Pekin Street #02-01
Far East Square
Singapore 048763

Printed in the United States of America.

Library of Congress Cataloging-in-Publication Data

Chapman, Carolyn, 1945-
Differentiated instructional strategies for writing in the content areas/Carolyn Chapman, Rita King. — 2nd ed.
      p. cm.
Includes bibliographical references and index.
ISBN 978-1-4129-7231-4 (cloth)
ISBN 978-1-4129-7232-1 (pbk.)
    1. English language—Composition and exercises—Study and teaching. 2. Language arts—Correlation with content subjects. 3. Individualized instruction. I. King, Rita. II. Title.

LB1576.C419 2010
372.62′3—dc22   2009012555

This book is printed on acid-free paper.

09   10   11   12   13   10 9 8 7 6 5 4 3 2 1

Acquisitions Editor:	Cathy Hernandez
Editorial Assistant:	Sarah Bartlett
Production Editor:	Libby Larson
Copy Editor:	Paula L. Fleming
Typesetter:	C&M Digitals (P) Ltd.
Proofreader:	Caryne Brown
Indexer:	Terri Corry
Cover Designer:	Rose Storey

CONTENTS

ACKNOWLEDGMENTS

Corwin gratefully acknowledges the contributions of the following reviewers:

Becky J. Cooke, Principal
Prairie View Elementary School
Spokane, WA

Margarete Couture, Principal
South Seneca Central School District
Interlaken, NY

Jolene Dockstader, Seventh-Grade Language Arts Teacher
Jerome Middle School
Jerome, ID

Barb Keating, Principal
FW Howay Community School
New Westminster, BC
Canada

Steve Knobl, Principal
Gulf High School
New Port Richey, FL

Linda Prichard, PreK–5 Instructional Specialist
Rutherford County Schools
Murfreesboro, TN

ABOUT THE AUTHORS

Carolyn Chapman continues her life's goal as an international educational consultant, author, and teacher. She supports educators in their process of change for today's students. She has taught in classrooms from kindergarten to college. Her interactive, hands-on professional development opportunities focus on challenging the mind to ensure success for learners of all ages. She believes all students *do* learn. Why not take control by putting excitement and quality into effective learning? Carolyn walks her walk and talks her talk to make a difference in the journey of learning in today's classrooms.

Carolyn authored *If the Shoe Fits . . . How to Develop Multiple Intelligences in the Classroom.* She has coauthored *Multiple Assessments for Multiple Intelligences, Multiple Intelligences Through Centers and Projects, Differentiated Instructional Strategies for Reading in the Content Areas, Differentiated Instructional Strategies: One Size Doesn't Fit All, Test Success in the Brain-Compatible Classroom, Differentiated Assessment Strategies: One Tool Doesn't Fit All, and Differentiated Instructional Management: Work Smarter, Not Harder.* Video Journal of Education Inc., features Carolyn Chapman in *Differentiated Instruction.* Carolyn's company, Creative Learning Connection Inc., has also produced a CD, *Carolyn Chapman's Making the Shoe Fit,* and training manuals to accompany each of her books. Carolyn has published multimedia kits for professional development and training, including *Differentiated Instructional Management, Differentiated Instructional Strategies for Reading in the Content Areas,* and *Differentiated Instructional Strategies for Writing in the Content Areas.* Each of these publications and her trainings demonstrate Carolyn's desire and determination to make an effective impact for educators and students. She can be contacted through the Creative Learning Connection Web site at www.carolynchapman.com.

Rita King, an educational consultant, conducts training sessions for teachers, administrators, and parents at local, state, and international levels. Her areas of expertise include multiple intelligences, practical applications of brain-based research, differentiated teaching and learning, reading and writing strategies, creating effective learning environments, and strategies for test success. Rita's sessions give educators and parents innovative, engaging activities to develop students as self-directed, independent learners. Participants enjoy Rita's practical, easy-to-use strategies, sense of humor, enthusiasm, and genuine desire to foster the love of learning.

Rita coauthored *Test Success in the Brain-Compatible Classroom, Differentiated Instructional Strategies for Reading in the Content Areas, Differentiated Assessment Strategies: One Tool Doesn't Fit All,* and *Differentiated Instructional Management: Work Smarter, Not Harder.* She also coauthored training manuals to accompany the books for professional development trainings. Rita has published multimedia kits for professional development and training, including *Differentiated Instructional Management, Differentiated Instructional Strategies for Reading in the Content Areas*, and *Differentiated Instructional Strategies for Writing in the Content Areas.* Rita can be contacted through her Web site, King Learning Associates, at www.kinglearningassociates .com, or by e-mail at kingrs@bellsouth.net.

INTRODUCTION 1

The Author's Flight

A young author develops writing wings.

Each takes a unique learning journey.

Each one writes the best that he can.

Why compare one against the other?

A writer is unique. Each passage is special.

An author's flight is limitless.

—Chapman and King, 2009 (adapted from
"A Butterfly in the Wind," author unknown)

INFUSING WRITING INTO THE CONTENT AREAS

Each student is a writer with unique needs. The way a teacher influences each individual's personal use of the writing craft affects the learner's writing destiny.

Effective teachers present writing as a tool for learning and expressing ideas (Schmoker, 2007). They share various forms of writing with their students to model and illustrate the purposes and the pleasures that come from content mastery and authorship. Productive writing instructors know how students learn. They preassess the students' strengths, abilities, and interests and use the results strategically to plan successful writing experiences. They choose strategies that jog the learner's mind to use higher-order critical-thinking skills and creativity.

Effective writing teachers clearly explain the guidelines, expectations, and evaluation procedures for each writing activity. Routine, specific feedback with appropriate guidance is provided. Writers are led to see errors as opportunities for improvement. All writing attempts are supported. Each success is genuinely praised.

Writing is used more today than ever. Young people are writing informally on a daily basis, using electronic tools such as e-mail, blogs, text messages, and personal Web pages. This intriguing type of writing often becomes an obsession for students. Educators need to build on this writing mania instead of downplaying these communication shortcuts. However, it is essential for students to learn how to apply the standards of writing in formal and informal situations.

Educators are urged to infuse writing into all content areas (National Commission on Writing, 2003). In each classroom, the teacher requires learners to have pencils and paper. Every instructor who gives writing assignments is a writing teacher. The activity may be very brief, such as writing a step-by-step procedure. Students need to see the relevant writing skills modeled daily and explained at each grade level and in all content areas.

Open-ended questions appear on many assignments as well as on tests. Often students know the information and can explain it to their peers. They bog down, however, when they try to place their thoughts on paper. A productive writer realizes, "If I can say it, I can write it." (Chapman & King, 2009, p. 2). Written work becomes a more accurate assessment of the learners' knowledge when they know how to write what they are thinking or saying to themselves.

DIFFERENTIATED WRITING INSTRUCTION

Differentiation is a philosophy that enables teachers to plan strategically in order to reach the needs of diverse learners in classrooms today to achieve targeted standards.

—Gregory & Chapman (2007, p. 2)

A major goal of education is for students to become self-directed learners as thinkers and productive problem solvers (Costa & Kallick, 2000). Differentiated instruction meets this need because each aspect of the individual is considered, including the student's intelligences, learning styles, and emotional states. In the differentiated writing classroom, teachers work with each student's unique needs. The goals for each learner include the following:

- To know how to apply information
- To think and write critically
- To think and write creatively
- To solve problems in the real world

These skills develop confident authors who are self-directed learners. To meet these needs, the teacher can differentiate the content, the instructional strategies and activities, the assessment tools, and the performance tasks (Gregory & Chapman, 2007).

Differentiating Content in Writing

- Break informational text writing assignments and materials into smaller chunks.
- Use simpler or more complex content vocabulary as needed.

- Tune into the learner's modalities to plan writing experiences with content information.
- Provide reference materials for writing at the student's reading level.
- Vary the genres in activities and assignments.
- Plan content area writing assignments according to the student's needs, as revealed in the assessment data.

Differentiating Assessment in Writing

- Collect writing samples to identify mastery of skills and standards.
- Vary assessment strategies.
- Use a variety of formal and informal assessment tools.
- Teach students how to use self-assessment tools.
- Use gathered data to plan for the learner's diverse needs.

Differentiating Performance Tasks in Writing

- Provide writing-task choices in the student's strongest learning styles and intelligences.
- Vary the ways students share their personal writing.
- Plan writing opportunities for students to show what they know.
- Use a variety of writing implements and materials.
- Form cluster teams to develop writing presentations.
- Challenge students to add writing to their projects and displays.

Examples:

captions	posters	portfolio entries	processing steps
procedures	explanations	fliers	summaries
banners	illustrations	graphic organizers	foldables

Differentiating Instructional Strategies

- Present writing activities that engage the students' unique learning modalities, styles, and intelligences.
- Plan writing activities in different genres.
- Use flexible grouping scenarios.
- Assign informal and formal writing assignments.
- Use a variety of writing activities with diverse topics and subjects.

We developed this resource to provide writing strategies for educators to use in daily plans along with textbook information and other resources to develop lifelong writers. We believe each idea, strategy, and activity can be used to assist learners in the diverse ways they process information for long-term memory, test success, and everyday use.

WRITING AND THE BRAIN

Making Mental Connections

According to David Sousa (2006), "Teachers try to change the human brain every day. The more they know about how it learns, the more successful they can be" (p. 3). The latest brain research provides information about the best approaches for engaging the student's mind for optimal learning. For instance, the learner's brain pays attention to personally meaningful information. When writing strategies are presented to link prior and new information with the student's practical world, the learner is more likely to remember and use it.

If the student has had prior experiences with a topic, mentioning the topic activates mental pictures and feelings. Consider the student's prior writing experiences in planning so new skills and strategies are based on the learner's experiences and level of understanding. (See, for example, the adjustable assignments in Figures 4.4, 5.7, and 5.8.)

Building Long-Term Memory

A student's ability to remember new information depends on previous knowledge (Willingham, 2006). Teachers plan new writing concepts and knowledge to make connections with the student's prior knowledge. New information is reconstructed to fit the learner's schema as it is stored in memory.

The writer needs to think about the best way to store learned information. Use the term *metamemory* to emphasize the importance of thinking about the memory strategy being used. Share the following with the students:

> *If I see the purpose,*
>
> *If I understand it,*
>
> *If I know how to use it,*
>
> *If I need it,*
>
> *I will remember it and use it.*
>
> —Chapman and King

Achieving a State of Flow

Csikszentmihalyi (1990) studied motivation and described optimal learning experiences as a state of flow. *Flow* is the state of mind that occurs when the student is totally immersed in a writing activity. In this state, the learner concentrates on the task at hand, enjoys it, and is not easily distracted. Individuals enter the state of flow while engaging in a favorite or high-interest writing activity. Flow does not occur when the learner is bored or frustrated. The desire to be involved is obvious in most students. Set the stage for the learner to enter into a state of flow by presenting challenging, successful writing experiences.

RATIONALE FOR WRITING IN THE CONTENT AREAS

Writers Write to Demonstrate Understanding

Teachers use writing assignments in content areas because they provide easy, quick assessments of a student's knowledge. There is not enough time to listen to each student's oral responses. Writing is one of the most efficient ways to check individual understanding (Fisher & Frey, 2007).

Writers Write to Enhance Learning and Memory

Writing activates memory as information enters the learner's schema and mental pathways. For information to enter long-term memory, the student has to connect prior experiences and current information to build new learning. Writing activities create these bridges, making it easier for learners to recall information for academic activities, including tests and daily use.

Writing is a tool for learning. The author identifies information stored in memory and organizes it so the reader or listener understands it. This mental processing provides the author with opportunities to think about the information as it is recalled and to think about it again while writing. Langer and Applebee's seminal research (1987) indicated that the kind of manipulation of content that occurs when students write leads to an increased understanding of that content.

Writers Write to Inform and to Express Important Ideas in the Real World

To make writing experiences meaningful, the student understands the value of the skill. The learner needs to see many ways to use it in his or her immediate world and the future role it will play. In the real world, writing is used to inform, to learn, and to express ideas. Use some of the following ideas about the many reasons writers write in a discussion to emphasize the importance of this skill:

- Analyze and solve problems.
- Express feelings, including anger, joy, laughter, or sadness.
- Share secrets, personal ideas, and interests.
- Share experiences, wildest ideas, and discoveries.
- Record information.
- Share thoughts with others.

- Appreciate the beauty and magic of language.
- Remember information for later use or study.
- Play with words, thoughts, and ideas.
- Relax and enjoy self-expression.
- Brainstorm and journal.
- Become a published author.

TURN ON THE WRITER

Most toddlers find joy in holding a pencil in their hands. After a few years, however, many students respond to writing activities and assignments as dreaded experiences. Why do these negative feelings develop? Many students receive negative feedback through grades and informal comments from adults. They become convinced that they cannot write. These learners build barriers to writing experiences because they fear failure.

In many classrooms, educators emphasize writing mechanics and the "look" of the work. However, writing involves complex problem-solving techniques, so more emphasis should be placed on getting the information on paper. The most valuable aspects of each writing experience are the content, the organization, and the author's style as an effective communicator.

Long, boring assignments turn off the learner's desire to write. Students are often turned off when they hear "Answer the questions at the end of the chapter," or "Write the list of words and the definitions." These writing assignments are viewed as the "same old, same old." It is a shame that the student's natural desire to write is turned off so easily. Educators need to be aware of emotional barriers and turn on enthusiasm for writing. Design each experience strategically for the learner to visualize himself or herself as a successful, productive writer. Remember, the student's attitude leads to altitude!

The chart in Figure 1.1 provides an overview of the writing tools and strategies included in this resource to meet young authors' needs, to turn on the writer, and to enrich the content information.

EVERY TEACHER IS A WRITING TEACHER: THE POWER IS YOURS!

Every class has writing assignments. It is not realistic for a teacher to say, "This is not a writing class. These students need to learn writing skills in language arts classes!" or, "If they have not learned the writing skills by now, they are not capable of learning them." All educators must assume these challenges.

Educators need to take an inventory of their personal feelings related to teaching young writers. According to Marjorie Frank in *If You're Trying to Teach Kids How to Write . . . You've Gotta Have This Book!* (1995) teachers need to understand their

Figure 1.1 An Overview of the Book: Differentiated Instructional Strategies for Writing in the Content Areas

Creating a Climate for Writing	Knowing the Writer	Differentiating the Writing Process and Flexible Grouping	Instructional Strategies and Activities	Planning, Assessing, and Evaluating Writing
Effective Writing Environment • Instill self-efficacy. • Develop internal motivation. • Develop self-regulated learners. A Safe and Positive Atmosphere • Slogans and poster ideas • The four Bs for writing • Assessing the affective writing environment A Physical Environment for Writing • Razzmatazz to thingamajigs • Cool tools • Material magic • Make the size fit. • Rainbow writing • Ready references • Teacher-created displays • Student-created displays Finding the "Write Spot" • Sensational stations Assessing the Physical Writing Environment	Stages of a Writer • Scribbler • Picture maker • Storyteller • Letter shaker • Copier • Sound maker • Sentence maker • Fluent writer Diagnosing the Writing Characters • Drawing Don • Insecure Inez • Plagiarizing Paul • Procrastinating Polly • Stumped Stan • Wordy Wilma • Refusing Randy • E. L. L. Ella • Author Arthur More Common Writing Problems and Interventions Learning Styles and Multiple Intelligences • Gardner's multiple intelligences theory • Sternberg's triarchic model • Student surveys	Types of Writing • Descriptive • Expository • Persuasive • Narrative • Using the Four Types The Block Party The Writing Process • Process the process. • Practice the process. Step 1. Getting Started: Prewriting Step 2. Sloppy Copy: First Draft Step 3. Hamming It Up: Revision Step 4. Tuning It Up: Editing Step 5. Neat Sheet: Final Copy Step 6. Publishing: Sharing and Celebrating Flexible Grouping T-Total group A-Alone P-Partner S-Small group	Teaching Each Writing Strategy Strategically Informational Text Writing and Critical Thinking Writing Strategies for English-Language Learners Formats and Genres Using Personification to Process Content Information Planning for Individual Needs • Choice boards • Agendas • Individualized writing projects • Language experience activities Writing Strategies • Brainstorming • Journaling Gathering Research • Proposals and contracts • Teacher's role • Student's role • Ways to research a topic • Presenting research with "zippidy-do" • Research conferences Note Taking • For listening • For reading • Research note cards Developing Outlines and Rubrics Writing Essays Rhymes and Riddles Getting to Know Text Characters Sequencing With Graphic Organizers Writing From A to Z	Lesson Planning Model • Before writing • During writing • After writing Effective Assessment Tools • Formal • Informal • Prepare for assessment scenes • Rubric for essays • Scales • Project rubric • Portfolios • Grading

7

"attitudes and beliefs, fears and abilities" (p. 19). An individual's self-efficacy, or belief in his or her success as a writing teacher, impacts the way the activities are approached. Each teacher has the power to change the quality of students' lives by giving them the writing skills they need for academic and personal success.

A Golden Opportunity

Each teacher has a golden opportunity to model and teach writing purposes and skills, as well as to make writing assignments fulfilling experiences for students. Textbooks and materials provide excellent facts and concepts to involve and challenge young authors. The activities expose learners to the different genres, styles, and types of writing in the real world. They grow in their ability to write with each experience in and out of the classroom. The teacher's passion for the subject is instilled in students through intriguing hooks, modeling, and meaningful writing activities. One teacher's interest can excite learners and build writing confidence and ability. Stimulating assignments motivate students to become fluent authors.

The strategies and activities in this resource were created by the authors or adapted from effective practices. Many lists, definitions, and activities are designed for the student to use. Words of encouragement, tips, and practical applications are included. Each writing tool is designed to enhance thinking and learning in differentiated classrooms.

Our Mission

Our mission is twofold: (1) to teach students how to use writing as an effective learning tool and (2) to encourage and assist all teachers as they use writing as a valuable component of differentiated instruction. Educators often target skills for writing improvement in daily lessons and test preparations. However, we seldom see students' self-satisfaction, enjoyment, empowerment, or confidence considered in formal plans. Explicitly state the purpose for each skill, strategy, or experience. Writers should find the activity appealing to have a desire to complete the task.

Refer to each writer as an *author*. The personal title will increase the learner's confidence. Throughout this guide, writers are referred to as authors. Each learner must believe in his or her ability as an author and know that each writing attempt will be respected and appreciated.

We hope the ideas presented are used and adapted to teaching information in all curriculum areas while developing successful, confident, enthusiastic authors.

*When a butterfly egg is hatched in a proper environment,
it has everything needed to thrive.*

When entering the writing world, most children possess
everything needed to become fluent authors.

ESTABLISHING THE
EFFECTIVE WRITING ENVIRONMENT

In a differentiated classroom, the climate is conducive to writing. It is a comfortable, exciting place for each young author. All aspects of the physical and psychological environment are established with the students' individual needs in mind. Lessons include activities that motivate and challenge with novel strategies, materials, and tools that intrigue the writers.

In supportive surroundings, young authors feel secure in taking risks with their ideas and skills during writing exercises. They view their mistakes as opportunities to improve, because errors are corrected with specific, positive feedback and encouragement. The teacher schedules ample time for the writers to complete assignments at their own pace (Barone & Taylor, 2006).

The students understand the value of writing for learning and communicating ideas. The teacher guides young authors to see the value of expressing emotions and thoughts in their unique styles. Writing experiences provide opportunities for the students to see themselves as authors. They develop a deep appreciation for published authors through exposure to a variety of genres. The teacher shares the joy of writing daily.

Instill Self-efficacy

Self-efficacy creates the "I believe in me!" feeling. The student needs to believe in his or her own writing ability. Self-efficacy is cultivated and instilled when specific, positive comments provide recommendations for improvement. Each writing experience is carefully planned to develop the student's belief that he or she is a successful author. Learners are defeated when they begin a writing experience without seeing its value or purpose, without clear directions, and with little or no background with the topic or skill. Each instructional segment is designed so the writer's self-doubt is replaced with self-confidence, the "I can . . ." feeling.

Develop Internal Motivation

The learner's enthusiasm, effort, and energy used to accomplish a task or participate in an activity are driven by internal motivation. Some factors involved in intrinsic motivation include self-determination, curiosity, challenge, and effort (Santrock, 2009; Stipek, 1996). The writer's internal goals are determined by the motivation or desire to achieve. Teachers nurture this desire to participate and to accomplish tasks. The excitement for learning subject matter is contagious. For example, when students are hooked by a teacher's character reenactment, they are anxious to write about the experience.

The individual's desire to associate with others or to work alone is considered in each lesson design. Strategically plan flexible groups to include time for total-group, independent, partner, and small-group writing activities. Build interest and curiosity by presenting choices. Create a team spirit to fulfill the learner's need to belong. Encourage the student to set personal learning goals for improvement. When an individual becomes self-directed or self-motivated, optimal learning occurs. Teachers fuel the learner's internal drive and zest for informational or creative writing.

Develop Self-Regulated Learners

The overall goal of the writing teacher is to develop self-regulated students who monitor and structure their thought processes to learn and communicate. They know how to think about their thinking.

Personal self-monitoring of one's thoughts is referred to as *metacognition*. Teachers guide students through the thinking processes that accompany writing experiences before, during, and after each activity. The student's thoughts are spoken, so the teacher can teach the self-monitoring process. When the learner demonstrates a thorough understanding of and ability to apply the strategy correctly and automatically, the teacher guides the writer to apply the skills silently.

Self-talk leads a learner through the thinking needed to complete tasks. For example, when several writing topics are presented as choices, students use self-talk to review their knowledge on the various subjects and select a familiar theme. Likewise, during a writing activity, the student knows how to use self-talk periodically to be sure sentences are in sequential order and support the main idea. After writing, the student knows to use a checklist to see that everything is complete. Learners need time and encouragement to apply metacognitive strategies as they apply and process new material.

Young authors must know and understand the thinking processes that accompany writing skills and strategies. Inspire self-regulated learning by modeling skills, customizing learning experiences, and exhibiting high expectations.

CREATING A SAFE AND POSITIVE WRITING ATMOSPHERE

In an emotionally safe writing environment, the authors' work is accepted. They know each piece of writing is special and is treated with respect. In this atmosphere, students are eager to participate in writing experiences. Create a personalized environment that motivates, challenges, and stimulates the authors' desire to write.

If a student has a red-mark phobia because errors have been emphasized, this student avoids writing, even when knowledgeable about the content. In a safe environment, on the other hand, each mistake is viewed as an opportunity to improve. The student needs time to correct individual work, to make needed improvements, and to share writing accomplishments.

The climate is nonthreatening, so students feel free to take risks. They have opportunities to express themselves in an atmosphere of open communication. Students who think "out of the box" are praised. Display sayings, charts, and other visuals to reflect positive expectations.

Slogans and Poster Ideas

- Write, Write, Write!

- We are authors. We write!

- We talk! We write! We share!

- If I can say it, I can write it!

- The more I write, the better author I will be!

The Four Bs for Writing (A Poster Example)

Be there.   Pretend you are in the scene.

Be brief.   Make words count. If you are too wordy, the message will be buried.

Be clear.   Express your thoughts with words everyone will understand.

Be positive.   Write your message in positive terms, especially when the context is negative.

In a safe environment, the uniqueness of each individual's writing is emphasized. The piece may be difficult to read; it may contain some incorrect word usage and mechanics. However, it is the author's writing. Teach the student to take pride in each writing experience. Build self-efficacy and confidence by giving the writer ownership. One way to accomplish this task is to ask the student to read his or her work orally and sign each piece as the author. For example, a writer signs, "Author, Susan Jones."

Assessing the Affective Writing Climate

Teachers set the tone that influences the students' feelings and emotions during writing periods. Use the assessment tool in Figure 2.1 to identify strengths and weaknesses to make a classroom or school an inviting place for writing experiences.

CREATING A PHYSICAL ENVIRONMENT FOR WRITING

The physical environment includes all tangible items in the classroom. It is where the teacher and students reside to carry out their tasks in teaching and learning. Some objects, such as the furniture, equipment, and display areas, are stationary. Most of the

Figure 2.1   Assessing the Affective Writing Climate

Place an X on the appropriate place on the line that describes the writing climate.

Elements of Acceptance in a Writing Classroom	Most of the Time	Rarely, If Ever
1. I provide a psychologically safe environment so students feel free to express ideas.	_____	
2. I think of writing activities from the student's point of view.	_____	
3. I model and share my writing experiences.	_____	
4. I respect writing time and avoid interruptions.	_____	
5. I emphasize the value of daily improvements more than grades.	_____	
6. I use specific praise to correct writing.	_____	
7. I encourage writing through my verbal and nonverbal behaviors.	_____	
8. I use open-ended questions to encourage divergent responses.	_____	
9. I vary genres in writing assignments.	_____	
10. I give encouragement to the struggling author.	_____	
11. I provide exciting writing opportunities within units of study.	_____	
12. I use specific constructive feedback when improvements are needed.	_____	
13. The student is given opportunities to share in various ways.	_____	
14. I provide ample time for writing with content information.	_____	
15. It is obvious to each student that I am excited about writing activities.	_____	

My improvement goal is _____.

I can improve the writing environment by _____.

resources and materials are temporary or consumable. The teacher designs the classroom with the students' learning styles, intelligences, talents, and interests in mind to enhance and customize their writing experiences.

The effective print-rich environment reinforces the content information being learned. Display student work to give each learner a sense of ownership. If you have more than one class, designate sections of the room for each group.

A print-rich environment includes the use of signs, labels, lists, and charts (Cox, 2008). One of the easiest ways to check your implementation of a print-rich environment is to stand in the classroom doorway when students are not present. Ask yourself if someone entering the room would know the topics, standards, skills, and objectives in the current study by viewing the writing displays and other visuals. A print-rich environment is essential at all grade levels. The displays serve as research data boards and reflections of student learning.

Provide an exciting writing environment so the student looks forward to the activities. Build anticipation into the experiences so the learner is eager to work with new topics. Use "unknowns" to intrigue and stimulate curiosity. Entice the student with novel writing instruments and materials.

Razzmatazz to Thingamajigs

Create a treasure trove of writing tools to intrigue young authors. Use writing instruments and materials related to the content to build interest and motivate students. Vary the size, color, and shape of the paper in activities and assignments. Match the materials to the assignment to enhance the content or to add novelty to the task. For example, while studying Japan, use rice paper. In a lesson about the Bill of Rights, use parchment paper.

Cool Tools

Vary the size, color, shape, and texture of writing implements. A student may feel more at ease writing with larger or smaller tools, an ink pen or pencil. The following Cool Tools list provides suggestions for novel writing implements. Add more instruments to the list to enhance content writing experiences.

Try These Cool Tools

Brushes	Chalk	Chocolate	Clay	Crayons
Dough	Glitter	Glue	Icing	Markers
Paint	Pebbles	Strings	Thread	Sand

Pens: colored, felt, gel, glitter, highlighter, calligraphy, ink, or quill

Pencils: fat, skinny, long, short, colored, graphite, or unique shapes and designs

Material Magic

Most writing assignments are completed on notebook paper. Add spice to activities by varying the medium, size, shape, color, weight, and texture of the writing materials. Correlate the materials with the topic of study. Using a variety of writing materials keeps students tuned in to topics and hooked on assignments.

Anticipation is a motivator. Generate curiosity with a variety of material magic. Use the following materials to capture the author's attention and ham up your teaching act:

construction paper	chalkboard	charts	parchment paper
dry-erase board	wallpaper	fabric	cards

cardboard	designed paper	index card	sticky note
sentence strip	newsprint	butcher paper	paper bag
shaving cream	pudding	lotion	adding machine tape
copy paper	neon paper	smart board	word processor
transparency	folder	T-shirt	text message device

Note: Ask a local print shop to save different types, sizes, textures, and colors of scrap paper. Also, newspaper offices often donate "end rolls" of newsprint. These sources provide the class with a variety of free paper for writing experiences.

Make the Size Fit

It is fun to fit writing assignments to various paper sizes. To choose the paper size, think about how much space the student needs to answer the question or complete the task. For example, if the response calls for a small bit of information, use a small piece of paper. Try a long, skinny piece for a list. Use a large piece of paper for group activities so everyone can work together and see the writing. Often, paper selected for size answers the old, familiar question "How much do I have to write?"

Use a shape directly correlated with the topic as a novel learning tool. The student links the information written with the design. For example, create a banner to display a logo, slogan, or goal to emphasize things to remember. Record nature facts on material shaped like a leaf, flower, or tree. Graphic organizers are popular learning tools that can be designed in various shapes related to the content.

The following ideas are presented to add novelty to the writing climate as students become engaged in folding, tearing, cutting, or shaping paper to fit the writing assignment.

Burrito Fold

Fold a sheet of paper into sections for the number of items needed. For example, use a burrito, or tri-fold, for three items or columns. Turn the paper vertically or horizontally to accommodate the information.

Suggestions for Use

- Write and/or draw the beginning, middle, and end of a story or procedure.
- Write and illustrate a three-step process.
- List or draw sorted items in three selected categories.
- Record individual responses of partners in the first two columns. They use the third section to summarize.
- Label the sections A, B, and C.
    a. Write notes from the reading assignment.
    b. Add notes from a small-group or class discussion.
    c. Write notes from a peer review before the test.

Accordion Fold

Fold a piece of paper to create four to six boxes as needed.

Suggestions for Use

Organize a number of

- problems to solve.
- paragraphs to summarize.
- vocabulary words to illustrate.
- categories.
- steps in a process, procedure, sequence, or recipe.

Hot Dog Fold

Fold a sheet of copy paper in half lengthwise to create a "hot dog." Tear along the fold and tape the two pieces of paper together to make one long piece. Fold the entire piece of paper in and out, making accordion creases. Students write on the front and back of the paper strip.

Suggestions for Use

- Write predictions on one side with facts on the other side.
- Place vocabulary words on one side and illustrations and meanings on the other side.
- Write a step-by-step process or procedure on one side with an example of each step in the sequence on the other side.
- List important facts to remember on one side with one or more supporting details on the other side.

High/Low Fold

Fold a piece of paper in half and draw a line on the crease.

Suggestions for Use

- Draw an important fact, symbol, or scene from the current study on the top half. Write details about the picture on the lower half.
- Solve a problem on the top half. Write the thinking process on the lower half.
- Draw a graphic organizer on the top section. Plot study details on the organizer. Create a passage using the information on the visual in the lower section.

The Shape of Things

Cut out a shape that represents an important item in the study. For example, use the outline of an octopus to record facts learned in an oceanography unit or use a rocket shape with a space study.

Suggestions for Use

- Write facts and supporting details on the shape.
- Write the name of an important person or a favorite character in the center. List the individual's attributes, contributions, or facts to create a border.
- Use shapes such as a circle, triangle, rectangle, or square in different colors if the content symbol is difficult to draw.

Quarter Tear

Give one student in a team of four members a sheet of paper to tear into four equal parts or sections. Instruct the learner to fold, crease, and tear the paper so each team member receives one section.

Suggestions for Use

- List facts or evidence of understanding as learning checkpoints
- Write a solution to a problem
- Respond to open-ended questions
- Create a summary statement
- Record facts from a passage
- Write reflection statements

Paper Stripping

Strip paper into the size needed for a list or specific information.

Suggestions for Use

- Brainstorm a list of ideas from individual students, partners, or small groups.
- Make a list and rank the ideas according to priority.
- Make a to-do list for a project, book report assignment, homework, materials needed, or agenda.

Sticky Tabbing

Tear the sticky portion of a sticky note into small pieces or tabs. Use the tabs to identify important information in the text, notes, or fact sheets.

Suggestions for Use

- Tab the main idea. Rewrite it on the remaining portion of the sticky note.
- Place the tabs on the supporting details. Write a prioritized list of the details.
- Tab important facts and events. Write the information in a favorite genre.
- Place tabs of one color on the nouns with tabs in another color on the verbs.
- Tab key words in a reading assignment. Write a summary using the tabbed words.

Rainbow Writing

Color stimulates the mind and evokes thoughts and feelings. Correlate colors with the topic. Provide color choices to bring out the student's best writing.

Suggestions for Use

- Record a historical battle on gray paper.
- Write a research study on oceanography using blue paper.
- Reflect on new learning using green paper to represent growth.

Ready References

Make various reference sources available so students have free access to them. Update and replenish materials as topics change. Ask students for suggested additions to the resource collection. The sources may include the following:

teacher notes	directions	pictures	word banks	books
dictionary	encyclopedia	time lines	charts	graphs
thesaurus	atlas	maps	magazines	brochure
Internet	computer software		pictionaries	video clips

Teacher-Created Displays

Make writing displays an integral part of the learning environment. Refer to the visuals to emphasize the value and usefulness of writing. The displays can be created through teacher-directed activities. Here are some ways to correlate writing with content lessons and daily activities.

Books	Labels	Directions	Schedules	Lists
• Supplementary books at individual reading levels • Books or booklets created by students • Reference books • Related literature	• Centers • Learning zones • Shelves • Supplies • Visuals • Exhibits • Personal items • Furniture • Displays • Charts • Time lines • Artifacts	• Rules • Activities • Experiments • Assignments • Routines • Guidelines • Assessments • Use of materials • Collecting work	• Topic outline • Events calendar • Center assignments • Special classes • Rotations • Conferences • Classroom roles • Order of dismissal • School events	• Goals • Important facts • Reference charts • Group roles • Class roll • Vocabulary • Procedures • Rules • Event order • Task order • Brainstorming

Student-Created Displays

Give students opportunities to display their own work. Doing so promotes a sense of belonging to the learning community. Whether you are a teacher with many classes or one group, remember that students need displays of what is being learned. Use the writing displays as places for gathering data on the current study or for reviews. When the study ends, move those artifacts to the hallway for more viewing and to use as reminders. This provides more space in the classroom for new learning displays.

Ways to Display

A print-rich environment includes the learner's writing. Here are some suggested spaces to display writing:

bulletin boards	doors	walls	shades	cabinet doors	halls
borders	smart boards	clotheslines	windows	stations	easels
ribbon	rope	yarn	chains	mobiles	banners

FINDING THE WRITE SPOT!

How many adults write letters or grocery lists while seated at a formal dining room table? Most people find a comfortable place to write. When individuals tire from sitting too long or experience writer's block, they move, stretch, engage in another task, go for a walk, or simply relax. Often thoughts for the writing task start floating around in the mind during the rest period. After the break, the writer returns with new ideas. This is what authors do!

Why are writing experiences at home so different from those at school? Do the experiences have to be different? No, in classrooms, authors can have seating choices, too. Some may spend hours seated at the computer composing documents. Others may choose to lie down with a laptop or a writing pad. After a long period, however, a comfortable spot often becomes very uncomfortable, and the physical need for a change becomes the student's priority. A break or change in position will usually refocus the mind and enhance the flow of ideas.

Sensational Stations

Designate special areas of the room as writing nooks, centers, zones, or stations. Use the centers for specific assignments or exploration. Give the activity an academic focus and purpose to connect with the content information. Design the writing station as a place for productive learning. If the student is wasting time, add relevant or high-interest activities. It may be necessary to post a sign over the area that reads, "Closed Until Further Notice!" Centers provide a place for the student to work on writing assignments alone, with a partner, or with a small group. Enhance learning and creativity in the sensational writing station with cool tools and material magic (see the preceding section of this chapter).

Create writing areas that correlate with units of study. For example, use a teepee during a study of Native Americans of the Great Plains or a table turned upside down to represent the boat George Washington used to cross the Delaware. "Write Spots" may contain sleeping bags, pillows from home, couches, or stuffed animals. A comfortable corner may have a special pillow, a reading lamp, a beanbag chair, or a soft rug. The student benefits from opportunities to choose or create a comfortable place to write. Of course, the teacher has final approval on the Write Spot.

ASSESSING THE PHYSICAL WRITING CLIMATE

Continually assess the learning environment to be sure materials and supplies are updated to intrigue writers. Display the students' work to create visual resources for current content lessons. Personal choice for seating, materials, and activities is a key to higher-quality writing performances. Use the checklist in Figure 2.2 to establish and maintain an effective writing climate.

Figure 2.2   Assessing the Physical Writing Climate: A Checklist
In my classroom, I . . .
❏ design the writing environment based on the learners' individual needs.
❏ customize the environment to enhance writing instruction.
❏ designate and label a special, comfortable, and appealing area for writing.
❏ identify areas for writing displays.
❏ post rules or guidelines as expectations in positive terms.
❏ display word lists.
❏ make "ready" reference books and materials accessible.
❏ make resources available on the students' reading levels.
❏ provide books and resources in the languages represented in the class.
❏ make materials and supplies accessible.
❏ plan lessons using various paper sizes, colors, textures, and shapes.
❏ provide students with opportunities to choose their writing implements and materials.
❏ provide art supplies, such as scissors and glue, for creative activities.
❏ make computers with word processing programs available.
❏ set up writing stations to reinforce and practice identified standards.
❏ designate display spaces with directions for students to post the work.
❏ provide cozy writing areas.
❏ play background music for added relaxation and to assist students in processing information.

SUMMARY

In differentiated classrooms, teachers encourage each young author to use individual talents, interests, and personality in writing activities and assignments. A student discovers the joy of writing through enjoyable experiences.

It is up to the teacher to establish and maintain a productive affective and physical learning environment to inspire each writer. A positive, stimulating writing climate motivates a student to become an author for a lifetime.

KNOWING THE WRITER 3

A butterfly evolves through developmental stages to become a beautiful, winged creature.

A student evolves through developmental stages to become an eager, fluent author.

STAGES OF A WRITER

Teachers observe authors as they evolve through developmental writing stages over time. Individual students may go through all the stages, or they may skip a stage. The stages may be identified in activities such as journal writing or other first-draft writing.

A writer evolves through developmental stages while engaging in appropriate writing experiences. At each stage, the student needs opportunities to develop through practice and experiments while receiving support and praise. With appropriate experiences, the writer has the potential to progress from the scribbler stage to the expertise of a distinguished author.

Students need acceptance as writers and acknowledgment as authors. If corrections for errors are nonthreatening, students are more likely to become fluent writers. The developmental writing stages are presented here with descriptions, characteristics, and teaching suggestions for younger and older students. In every productive differentiated classroom, the teacher recognizes and honors the diverse stages of writers.

Scribbler

Scribblers make bold marks haphazardly on their papers to create stories. These marks, with straight and curving lines, are the first signs of writing. The marks express the student's feelings and ideas. At this stage, the child imitates writing modeled by parents, siblings, teachers, friends, and other individuals. During scribbling experiences, the child's muscles are developing to hold the writing implement, eye-hand coordination is strengthening, and attitudes toward writing are forming.

Sometimes a scribbler identifies and describes the marks. For example, a child may scribble with various colors and say, "This is my car." If the adult responds, "Tell me about your car," this acceptance and praise encourages the scribbler to tell a story about the marks.

The Younger Student

As a child enters the world of writing, give the youngster numerous opportunities to use crayons, markers, and pencils to develop the fine motor skills he or she will use when formal writing begins. The young author needs a wide variety of experiences with cool tools before the first school experience (see "Razzmatazz to Thingamajigs" in Chapter 2). The child should be taught the proper places to experiment with writing, such as on paper, a chalkboard, or a dry-erase board. Praise the student for all marks made in appropriate places. Children who have no writing experiences before school need opportunities to see writing modeled daily. They need to develop fine motor skills and use their writing interests.

The Older Student

An older student may be in the first developmental writing stages. This individual may not enjoy writing because of previous failures. This learner may draw a scribbled line or a slash mark for an unknown word or phrase. An English-language learner is often in this stage. Letter symbols are used to write in the new language. The scribbles, representing words from the native language, are interspersed with mastered English words. The older scribbler moves beyond this stage with acceptance, encouragement, and assignments on his or her level of success.

Picture Maker

The picture maker expresses ideas in picture form. The design represents a personal interpretation of the learning or event. The student draws and tells a detailed story. Letters or numbers often appear interspersed in the drawing. The teacher encourages the student by saying, "Tell me about your drawing."

The Younger Student

The picture maker draws as a form of writing. This student does not know the alphabet or the appropriate letter combinations to form words. The drawings express thoughts without words. It may be difficult for adults to recognize forms represented in the pictures, but the child knows each detail and can tell a story using each one. To encourage elaboration and emphasize details, lead the child to tell more about the drawing through statements and questions like the following:

- Tell me about your picture.
- What can you add to your picture?
- Wow! What do you know about it?

An effective activity to use with a student at this stage is to fold a piece of paper in half. Ask the student to draw a picture with crayons on the top section. Instruct the student to put the crayons away and turn the paper to the bottom half. Give the learner time to write a story with a pencil on the bottom half. Tell the student to open the paper so both the drawing and the writing can be seen and have the student read the story aloud to a partner or to the teacher. The teacher has the option for creating a language experience as the child tells the story. If this option is chosen, the teacher says, "I am going to write the words you say as you tell me about your picture." As the child relates the story, the teacher writes the words in a separate place so the author's writing is not disturbed. The student sees writing modeled as the thoughts appear in words on paper. The student follows each word as the teacher reads and writes the story. During this experience, the child develops the concept that the picture and words tell the story.

The Older Student

An older student who finds it difficult to write his or her thoughts may be able to record ideas in picture form. This visual thinker sees ideas as mental pictures. When given the opportunity first to visualize and capture the mental images and then draw a picture before the writing experience, this student creates a more complete story. Use questions and prompts to help the student see the mental pictures clearly. When details are added to the picture, more details appear in the writing. Remember, a picture maker works well with graphic organizers. Teach this artistic learner to think it, see it, and draw it before writing.

Storyteller

A storyteller tells the story well. However, this student writes familiar letters and numbers randomly in a scribble form. It may be difficult or even impossible for the teacher to decode and read the symbols, but the student can tell a story by looking at the recorded symbols. This learner mimics the writing of other individuals.

The Younger Student

Allow time for the storyteller to write, even though an observer may not be able to read the message. As the student reads and tells the story, write the student's words to model writing. This continues the practice of writing the young author's story as demonstrated in the picture maker stage. Another way to meet the storyteller's needs is to provide a time and place for the student to record the story on a cassette, listen to it, and then write it. Remind the student to write the words as they are heard.

The Older Student

An older storyteller can tell the story or answer an open-ended question orally but has trouble placing the words on paper. This learner needs someone to write the story so the words are modeled and come to life.

The Storyteller and Invented Spelling

Encourage the storyteller to use invented spelling. Doing so produces more details and gives opportunities for elaboration. When the student has to concentrate on spelling, frustration may cause a loss of interest in the story. Invented spelling encourages the writer to use words that are difficult to spell. When conventional spelling rules are enforced the student often chooses words that are easy to spell. Acceptance of invented spelling fosters creativity and higher-order thinking skills, because the writer is able to focus on the content and organizing thoughts.

Letter Shaker

The letter shaker is beginning to recognize letter-sound associations. This is a very important writing stage. The student represents a word using mastered letter sounds. The words are composed of a few letters. The reader occasionally identifies familiar or correctly spelled words.

The Younger Student

The younger letter shaker relates to written symbols in the environment. The student may not know the difference between letters and words but understand connections between letters and their sounds. The letter shaker often points to a letter and says a word while telling the story. This behavior appears when the letters are being introduced with their sounds. After the student writes a story, the teacher writes the story as the child tells it. When a letter or word is recognized in the letter shaker's writing, the teacher draws a line from the letter or word in the story to the student's representation of the word. The child is praised for correct letters or words.

Copier

The copier writes words from the environment to pretend that a story is being written. In this stage, the child is linking phrases and sentences to the act of writing.

The Younger Student

The copier uses available words or sentences to pretend to be a writer. For example, the child may look at a bulletin board and copy the title "Fall is here!" and then write and tell an unrelated, personal story. The author is the only one who can read the work. The copier realizes that words are used to write a story.

As the copier develops, a print-rich environment is needed with vocabulary displays such as word walls, posters, and labeled objects. Give the young author access to resources such as dictionaries and pictionaries. A student at this stage benefits from using a rebus or labeled pictures.

The Older Student

The older student copies printed material from various resources and claims it as his or her writing. This learner knows the words must be placed on paper but lacks the confidence or desire to write in his or her own words. Often this student does not comprehend the written words. Explain the consequences of plagiarism. Teach the step-by-step writing procedures for note taking.

Sound Maker

The sound maker understands the letter-and-sound connection. This understanding is obvious when important parts of words are written using mastered decoding skills and syllabication strategies. The writer uses the sounds to form words. This becomes a time-consuming task.

The Younger Student

The younger sound maker writes the sounds heard in a word. Usually, the letters represent sounds from the beginnings and ends of words. This student is able to read the words aloud. This is the initial stage of invented spelling. Typically, the student no longer creates long stories to tell. The author strategically reads the words represented with letters. This is a beginning stage for accurate reading of personal writing.

A picture guides the sound maker to stay on the main idea. While reading the story, the student says the words represented by the letters. Allow the learner to point to the letters so the reading and writing connection is made. Write the story for the sound maker. Draw a line from the letter in the word to the letter used by the student. Give the student praise for using a letter in the word. For example, if the student writes the letters *ihab* and says, "I have a ball," draw a line from each letter to the word it represents in the sentence.

The Older Student

The older student using invented spelling is a letter shaker on a higher level. This student knows the letter sounds or some letters in the word. When this learner comes to a difficult word to spell, the letters heard and remembered are written. Invented spelling allows an author to write without interrupting the flow of thoughts.

Sentence Maker

The sentence maker writes sentences about the topic and uses invented spelling. Usually, these sentences relate to the main idea. This writer understands that personal words create thoughts and tell a story. This applies to the younger *or* older student's writing world. The skills and tools of mechanics used correctly demonstrate mastery. For example, when a student uses the correct punctuation mark at the end of a sentence, the skill is mastered and becomes a component of the student's knowledge base.

Fluent Writer

A fluent writer uses a personal style of writing to organize the story's content with a beginning, middle, and end. The reader easily follows the flow of thoughts created with a main idea and supporting details. The mastered skills and mechanics of writing are applied automatically. For example, mastered spelling words appear correctly in the writing. The fluent writing stage is found in the writing of younger *and* older students. This student yearns to share because writing is a rewarding, pleasant experience. Praise, honor, and celebrate the author's success.

Writing Stages: A Summary

Writing stages are developmental. To identify a specific stage, look through a variety of writing samples. A student may remain in one stage for a longer period than other writers. Older students who are reluctant writers, English-language learners, and special needs students may be identified as being in one of the writing stages. The student usually moves automatically to the next stage when exposed to writing modeled by adults and strategically planned writing opportunities.

DIAGNOSING THE WRITING CHARACTERS

Teachers in the content areas are often the first to observe a student's writing problems. The following descriptions identify observable behaviors teachers are likely to encounter during writing tasks in the differentiated classroom. The feelings commonly evident in struggling writers need to be recognized and respected by teachers, parents, and peers. The suggested interventions assist the teacher in solving each writing problem. With appropriate guidance, most students overcome obstacles and become fluent writers.

Drawing Don

Observable Behaviors

- Enjoys drawing.
- Shows what is known in pictures.
- Replaces a word or phrase with a symbol or sketch.
- Draws when given a choice.
- Uses doodling often.

Feelings of the Student

- I like to draw. If I draw first, I write better.
- I would rather draw than write.
- Drawing helps me understand what I have to learn.
- I like to work with a partner or a small group so I can draw on the poster.

Suggested Interventions

- Praise picture making as a writing stage.
- Encourage drawing as a prewriting activity.
- Provide a variety of art supplies.
- Allow the author to illustrate the writing.
- Accept drawings as options for writing assignments.
- Teach and encourage the writer to create graphic organizers to plot information and organize thinking.

Insecure Inez

Observable Behaviors

- Does not believe she can write.
- Lacks confidence.
- Has the ability to write but becomes easily frustrated.
- Is shy about sharing her work.

Feelings of the Student

- I'm afraid I will fail.
- I want to please everyone.
- My last writing assignment had red marks all over it.
- I cannot write like my friends.
- I don't want others to make fun of my writing.
- My writing always embarrasses me.

Suggested Interventions

- Conference with the writer to discuss and target the insecurities.
- Give short assignments that ensure success.
- Use specific praise and encouragement.
- Teach the student how to use self-praise statements.
- Assign topics that target favorite subjects.
- Assign a partner whom the writer trusts.
- Provide choices in activities, tools, and topics.

Plagiarizing Paul

Observable Behaviors

- Copies exact wording instead of writing the information in his own words.
- Lacks confidence and belief in his own writing.
- Does not know how to interpret the information.
- Does not think he will get caught.

Feelings of the Student

- I do not know what this means, so I will just copy it.
- It is easier just to copy the information.
- I will not use the word right.
- I don't know how to organize my ideas.

Suggested Interventions

- Teach plagiarism rules and laws.
- Demonstrate how to write information in the student's own words.
- Build the writer's confidence in his own thoughts and ideas by verbally expressing specific praise for each small success.

Procrastinating Polly

Observable Behaviors

- Is slow to finish.
- Wastes time.
- Is easily distracted during tasks.
- Lacks confidence.

Feelings of the Student

- I'll be the last one to finish.
- Everyone always tells me to "hurry up" or "stop wasting time."
- I would rather do anything other than write.
- I wish teachers would let me write about a subject that I know.
- I am interested in many things but not this assignment.
- I don't want to write because I don't know very much about this topic.

Suggested Interventions

- Begin with brief assignments.
- Provide guided practice with continuous feedback.
- Use a timer.
- Assign a writing partner who stays on-task.
- Allow choices for writing activities, seating, and supplies.
- Select high-interest topics.
- Use story starters or prompts.

Stumped Stan

Observable Behaviors

- Stops to spell correctly.
- Experiences writer's block.
- Shows fear of failure; says, "I do not like this."
- Waits for help.
- Is off-task often.
- Exhibits learned helplessness created by dependence on the thinking of the teacher, classmates, parents, or other adults.

Feelings of the Student

- I can't write any more until I find out how to spell this word.
- I can't think of anything to write for this next part.

- I just looked at that last night, but now I can't remember it.
- I feel frustrated. I wish I could write like my friends.
- I'm afraid I will be wrong.
- I get so embarrassed during writing time.

Suggested Interventions

- Develop knowledge and experiences with the topic prior to writing assignments.
- Build confidence with specific, positive feedback.
- Provide guided practice.
- Plan strategically for the writer's success in each writing experience.
- Explain the purpose of the first draft.
- Use prompts, including pictures.
- Plan prewriting activities so the student can collect thoughts and organize information.
- Allow extra time to complete work.

Wordy Wilma

Observable Behaviors

- Is redundant.
- Uses run-on sentences.
- Rambles, going on and on.
- Tries to use "big" words.
- Repeats thoughts in several ways.

Feelings of the Student

- I can tell that people do not like the way I express my thoughts.
- I have to give all the details so readers will understand.
- I am not a good writer.

Suggested Interventions

- Model quality writing.
- Provide an effective prewriting activity.
- Ask her to identify the main idea and supporting details.
- Use an organizer to gather and outline thoughts.
- Draw lines through unnecessary words, phrases, and sentences in the first draft.
- Record the student telling her thoughts. Ask her to listen to the recording and write the exact words she used.
- Teach the student to tell the story aloud before writing it.

Refusing Randy

Observable Behaviors

- Refuses to write.
- Exhibits a negative attitude.
- Shows no interest.
- Avoids all activities that involve writing skills.
- May have a negative verbal outburst.

Feelings of the Student

- I hate to write.
- I am not going to be successful, so I don't need to do this.
- I do not want to be the group recorder.
- I want to tell it rather than write it.

Suggested Interventions

- Give choices.
- Plan short writing assignments using small pieces of paper.
- Encourage the student to draw or make lists.
- Assign a partner who can script his thoughts.
- Hook the student on the topic.
- Use informal writing.
- Accept invented spelling.

E. L. L. Ella

Observable Behaviors

- Speaks and writes in the native language.
- Exhibits feeling of insecurity.
- Constantly tries to understand what others are doing, saying, or writing.
- Avoids all activities that involve writing skills.
- May have a negative verbal outburst.

Feelings of the Student

- I don't understand what I am to do.
- No one understands me.
- I am not going to be successful.
- I do not want to be the group recorder.
- I wish I could tell about it in my own language instead of writing it.

Suggested Interventions

- Make the learner comfortable during all writing experiences.
- Accept some writing in the native language.
- Give short writing assignments on small pieces of paper.
- Encourage the student to draw and use graphic organizers.
- Permit the student to make lists.
- Assign a partner who can script the writer's thoughts.

Author Arthur
Observable Behaviors

- Enjoys writing.
- Is a creative and confident writer.
- Sees himself as an author.
- Writes for pleasure.
- Enjoys sharing with others.

Feelings of the Student

- I like to write. It is one of my favorite things to do.
- I am an author.
- I have so many ideas I want to write.
- I like to write in my favorite genres.
- I make lists and set goals.
- I enjoy writing e-mails, text messages, and letters to my friends.
- I take notes to remember important information.

Suggested Interventions

- Provide positive writing opportunities.
- Encourage. Do not squelch enthusiasm.
- Give choices.
- Expand and enrich the student's areas of interest in writing activities.
- Provide publishing opportunities.

One of the most common problems faced by teachers in writing lessons is dealing with the student who refuses to write. Have a private conference with the student. Ask the learner to describe his feelings related to writing. Listen to the student's view or self-analysis. Use the information to plan writing opportunities to target the learner's needs. Design specific steps for overcoming the writing barriers.

MORE COMMON WRITING PROBLEMS AND INTERVENTIONS

Figure 3.1 lists common writing problems with some suggested interventions for improving individual writing performances.

From time to time, students exhibit writing problems in the content areas. Provide authors at all levels with praise and some form of recognition for their writing efforts. Remember to seek more suggestions and solutions for writing problems through discussions with colleagues and writing specialists in your school or district.

Figure 3.1 Common Writing Problems	
Problem	*Suggested Interventions*
Is unfamiliar with the topic.	• Provide the background needed by sharing artifacts, visuals, and related vocabulary words. • Give the learner resources and materials for learning about the topic. • Place the student in a discussion group to increase prior knowledge. • Change the assignment to a familiar topic if there is not enough time to build prior knowledge. • Brainstorm a list of topics to provide choices.
Lacks prewriting skills.	• Teach and model prewriting skills. • Model brainstorming. • Use partner or small-group brainstorming. • Provide a variety of strategies for the student to use to gather and record prewriting thoughts.
Mumbles while writing.	• Move to an area away from others. • Allow mumbling, if it is not disturbing anyone. • Model silent reading. • Praise when the student reads quietly.
Has difficulty beginning the first draft.	• Accept writer's block. • Allow the student to create a list of related words as an alternate activity. • Use writing prompts and questions. • Return to the prewriting stage strategies. • Provide topic choices. • Give the student time to talk about the topic.
Lacks depth on the assigned topic.	• Ask probing questions. • Go back to prewriting strategies. • Show the student how to reread the writing and add details. • Provide more time for research. • Show the student how to add missing pieces.

LEARNING STYLES AND MULTIPLE INTELLIGENCES

A student's learning style is the individual's preferred way to use his or her abilities. Each student has many preferences for learning. The most common learning style models include (1) auditory, (2) visual, (3) kinesthetic, and (4) tactile, or hands-on, learning. When learning styles are addressed in planning, one student may learn the steps in the writing process by creating a rap with a partner, while another student may prefer to work alone and design a graphic organizer to learn the steps.

Gardner's Multiple Intelligences Theory

While studying how the brain works, Dr. Howard Gardner developed the theory of multiple intelligences (1983). This theory shows that every brain has unique areas of strengths and weaknesses. Everyone has three to four strong areas. Weak areas can be strengthened, and everyone becomes more intelligent through personal experiences, interests, and life's opportunities. Teachers can use eight of Dr. Gardner's intelligences to label targets in lesson plans, such as designing a visual assignment of creating a collage. The activity or strategy is labeled, not the students. They have enough labels!

Gardner's eight intelligences targeted in classrooms are the following:

Verbal/Linguistic: Using language for communication with reading, writing, listening, speaking, and linking information

Musical/Rhythmic: Being sensitive to and using rhythm, beat, pitch, tone, timbre, and inflection

Logical/Mathematical: Solving problems and abstract thinking, using the number and pattern world

Visual/Spatial: Exploring art and all media, working with colors, visualizing and interpreting spatial relationships

Bodily/Kinesthetic: Using movement, touch, tactile, and hands-on learning; using the mind/body relationship

Naturalist: Adapting and surviving in one's world, studying and labeling nature, understanding and using nature in a personal way

Intrapersonal: Working alone, setting personal goals, using self-directed or personalized learning

Interpersonal: Working, socializing, empathizing, and/or cooperating with other people

The multiple intelligences theory impacts instruction, because teachers teach in their strongest intelligence areas. When teachers use their weaker intelligence areas in a lesson, they are working in areas of discomfort. However, it is important for teachers to do whatever is necessary to reach a student. It may be necessary to teach in a zone of discomfort to engage a student's area of strong intelligence.

Sternberg's Triarchic Model

Dr. Robert Sternberg studies the brain and how it works and has developed a model of successful intelligence that focuses on a triarchy of thinking abilities. "*Analytical ability* is used when a person analyzes, evaluates, compares, or contrasts. *Creative ability* is used when a person creates, invents, or discovers. *Practical ability* is used when a person puts into practice, applies, or uses what he or she has learned [emphasis added]" (Sternberg & Grigorenko, 2007, p. 10).

Sternberg believes each individual learns using these three ways of thinking. One or two of the intelligences may be dominant areas. For example, an analytical learner usually excels in traditional academic programs. Use Sternberg's theory to expand your knowledge of how a student approaches a writing task or a challenge.

Sternberg's intelligences have been adapted to create a planning tool, the triarchic teaming model (Chapman & King, 2008). Use it to design writing lessons that support the learner's strongest intelligences. For example, when forming groups for writing projects, assign at least one member with each intelligence to every group. This creates teams of individuals who approach the writing task from at least three thinking perspectives.

Student Surveys

The surveys shown in Figures 3.2 and 3.3 guide students to identify and understand their feelings and attitudes related to writing. It is important for learners to analyze and express their emotions to build confidence. Teachers can use the results to identify students who need specific activities to develop the positive attitudes necessary to generate interest in writing. The best surveys are designed by the teacher for an individual or specific group of students. Adapt the following surveys for specific groups.

Figure 3.2   Revealing Feelings
1. When I am told to write, I usually feel _____. Why?
2. I am a _____ writer because _____.
3. I learned to write when _____.
4. People write because they want to _____.
5. A good writer _____.
6. When others help me with writing, I feel _____.
7. When I help others with their writing, I feel _____.
8. The worst writing assignment I have to do is _____.
9. I like to write when _____.
10. My favorite writing topics are _____.

Figure 3.3   Attitude Analysis: A Writer's Self-Check

The following rubric is an informal assessment of a student's attitude toward writing experiences. The "scrimmage line" represents the low end of the scale; the "goalpost" represents the high end of the scale. The learner places an X on the scale beside each item. A few statements are prompts for the student to complete.

1. I enjoy writing.   Scrimmage Line .... Goalpost

2. Writing is easy for me.   Scrimmage Line .... Goalpost

3. I plan my writing.   Scrimmage Line .... Goalpost

4. I revise my work several times.   Scrimmage Line .... Goalpost

5. I read my work to myself.   Scrimmage Line .... Goalpost

6. I enjoy reading my writing
   to a partner.   Scrimmage Line .... Goalpost

7. I enjoy being an author.   Scrimmage Line .... Goalpost

8. The best thing about writing is _____.

9. To be an effective writer, I must have _____.

10. The worst thing about writing is _____.

11. My favorite place to write is _____.

12. When I write the answer to a discussion question, I _____
    _____.

SUMMARY

The more a teacher knows about each student as a writer, the easier it is to tailor writing experiences. A student with a writing problem is observed and diagnosed.

Use surveys often to know your students thoroughly. Use the information to plan specific activities for the unique needs of differentiated learners. Intervene with activities and assignments with the tools and opportunities for the writer to become a successful communicator.

DIFFERENTIATING THE WRITING PROCESS AND FLEXIBLE GROUPING 4

A butterfly emerges from the cocoon, spreads its wings, and flies.

A student automatically using writing skills and strategies is soaring as a young author.

IMMERSE STUDENTS IN THE WRITER'S CRAFT

A *craft* is an art or skill. Teach students about the value of writing as a craft. This includes where authors obtain information, how they conduct research, and how they create drafts. Teachers and students must understand and practice the how-tos of writing (National Commission on Writing, 2003). Learners must know how to apply the skills effectively in all content areas.

Young authors need to develop a writing vocabulary to discuss their writing. These terms include *draft, revise, edit,* and *publish.* They become familiar with the language of writing through sharing and discussing their work. Invite local authors to share their work and advice with students to give them meaningful connections to the vocabulary of the writer's craft.

Students are introduced to the many different forms of writing appropriate to different content areas. They move through the six steps of the writing process and immerse themselves in the writer's craft.

TYPES OF WRITING

Four types of writing are presented in this section with suggested teaching guidelines. Teach students to use the sentence in the heading for each type of writing to guide understanding and self-talk.

Descriptive Writing: Let Me Create a Picture in Your Mind!

Descriptive writing uses words to create images or impressions of a person, place, concept, object, or event. The student chooses words to activate the mind's eye, or visualization. The writer needs to grow in the ability to use descriptive language. This learning process develops over time through extensive practice and purposeful instruction within units of study. Begin descriptive writing experiences with simple assignments; for example, asking the student to describe familiar things in the environment. It is easier for the student to apply this skill to personal experiences, because the student's memories create the mental images. Other types of writing use some elements of descriptive writing. (For tips on writing with style, see Step 3 in the writing process, which deals with revision.)

To use descriptive writing, the learner should

- have background knowledge of the chosen topic.
- know how to express thoughts using a personal word bank.
- use adjectives, adverbs, and verbs effectively.
- understand how words activate the reader's senses.
- know how to explain the actions of characters and objects.
- use words to express and share ideas.
- be able to create pictures and images in his or her own mind.
- describe images so the reader can create mental pictures

Descriptive Writing Examples

Character analyses   Play scripts   Poetic descriptions   Comparisons/contrasts

Expository Writing: Let Me Explain It to You!

Expository writing informs with an explanation or report. It may involve giving a step-by-step account or a how-to procedure or reveal the causes of an event. Expository writing is found in training books, assembly manuals, recountings or explanations of an event, and retellings of stories. Key words used in some expository writing include *first, second, then, next,* and *finally.*

To use expository writing, the learner needs to know

- the meaning of informing and explaining.
- how to explain the order of an event, procedure, or process.
- ways for be specific and accurate in explanations.
- strategies of writing for readers who may retell the information or follow the procedure step-by-step.

Expository Writing Examples

Book report	Directions	Research paper	How-to guide
Instructions	News story	Recounting of an event	Informational text
Training manual	Procedure	Factual response	Scientific discovery

Persuasive Writing: Let Me Convince You!

Persuasive writing is the author's attempt to change the beliefs or behaviors of an individual or group of people. The writer uses words and phrases to persuade the reader or audience to adopt new ideas, behaviors, or other changes.

The author states an opinion and provides facts and details that explain, prove, or support it. The conclusion summarizes or restates the writer's beliefs. Students enjoy expressing opinions and ideas, so persuasive writing is an excellent tool to use when processing information. For example, young authors enjoy inventing new ways to use objects or ideas and creating persuasive passages to sell the products. Give students a form like the one presented in Figure 4.1 to structure their thoughts before writing.

Figure 4.1   Persuasive Writing Form

Topic _____

Name _____ **Date** _____

My Opinion

My Supporting Facts or Ideas

1.
2.
3.

Step Procedure

Step 1	**Process Thinking**
Step 2	**Process Thinking**
Step 3	**Process Thinking**
Step 4	**Process Thinking**

To use persuasion in writing, the learner should

- know how to state the opinions and beliefs.

- understand how words change, or sway, the beliefs of the readers.

- become aware of personal feelings and convictions of other people.

- demonstrate logical thinking and problem-solving skills in making decisions.

- realize that ideas, beliefs, rules, and laws can change by rewriting phrases, sentences, or sections.

Persuasive Writing Examples

Book review	Brochure	Commercial	Business letter
Editorial	Movie review	Poster	Letter to the editor
Position statement	Campaign speech	Critique	Advertisement

Narrative Writing: Let Me Tell You What Happened!

A narrative tells a story. It may be about an event in the present, past, or future. It may be fiction or nonfiction. The passage may be in various forms, including diaries, chapter books, short stories, essays, plays, tall tales, or legends.

To use narrative writing, the learner should

- know how to tell a story.

- write as if telling the story or information to someone.

- develop a beginning to introduce the characters, scene, and problem.

- develop characters and actions throughout the passage.

- create an ending that restates the main idea or purpose with a solution and conclusion.

Narrative Writing Examples

Biography	Diary	Fantasy	Fable	Historical fiction
Legend	Mystery	Myth	Novel	Current event
Tall tale	Play	Story	Sitcom	Science fiction

Using the Four Types of Writing

The chart in Figure 4.2 outlines the purposes and features of the four types of writing with a few assignment examples for each one. Encourage the student to use Figure 4.3 as a reference tool when using the four types of writing. Place the form in the individual's writing portfolio.

Figure 4.2 Types of Writing	
Descriptive Writing	*Expository Writing*
Purpose: To picture	**Purpose:** To inform
Features • Uses adjectives, adverbs, and active verbs. • Uses sensory words. • Shows instead of telling. • Uses figurative language, such as metaphors and similes. • Creates vivid mental pictures.	**Features** • Recounts or retells using *who, what, when, where,* and *why*. • Gives details. • Shows or tells step by step. • Describes a procedure. • Explains "how to."
Examples • Describe a place, person, object, or event. • Visualize a picture in one's mind. • Write a story, poem, report, or essay.	**Examples** • Tell what happened for a news program. • Record the event in a diary. • Explain the procedure. • Retell the story. • Write a recipe or news flash.
Narrative Writing	*Persuasive Writing*
Purpose: To tell	**Purpose:** To convince
Features • Gives details of characters, plot, setting, and events. • Tells who, what, when, and where, how, and why. • Has a strong storyline. • Shows sequence of events. • States problems, complications, or dilemmas. • Defines or tells about _____.	**Features** • Strives to change the audience's thinking. • States a point of view. • Tells what and why. • Has a specific audience. • Gives the expert's and believer's position. • States position with support. • Contains a closing argument.
Examples • Tell about an event, place, person, or thing for a newspaper. • Write a fiction or nonfiction story for a school newspaper.	**Examples** • Give a speech to convince the audience that _____. • Write an editorial to express your feelings about _____. • Write an article for a brochure to win the reader over to your side of an issue.

THE BLOCK PARTY

The block party activity is designed to meet the diverse needs of students as they practice four types of writing. It also serves to help students practice the writing process. Assign responsibilities and roles using their learning preferences and areas of strength related to their intelligences. Each student in a four-member team is assigned one type of writing with a graphic organizer to gather ideas. All team members brainstorm ideas to complete each individual's organizer. After all organizers are filled with ideas, each team member writes a brief essay or story using his or her assigned type of writing. At the completion of this activity, each group has four prewriting activities and four first drafts representing the four types of writing.

Figure 4.3	Types of Writing: A Reference Tool	
Type of Writing	*Purpose*	*Details*
Narrative	Tells	• Completes a plot or story. • Provides interesting information. • Uses dialogue. Examples: story, legend, tall tale
Descriptive	Describes	• Paints a picture using words. • Creates emotional connections. • Uses vivid adjectives, adverbs, and figurative language. • Uses dialogue. Examples: diary, account
Persuasive	Convinces	• Answers a potential question with supporting details. • Sways to one side of an issue. • Expresses positive opinion. Examples: ad, editorial, platform
Expository	Informs	• Addresses topic with important details and facts. • Gives information the reader needs to know. • Explains in clear and concise language. Examples: news article, informational guide

Materials

Each group needs of four sheets of copy paper, five index cards, and four pencils.

Part I

1. Take a sheet of paper and a pen or pencil to meet your partner.

2. Join another partner team to form a cooperative group with four members and find a comfortable place to work.

3. Sit with two members facing two members to form the block party.

4. Choose a Captain and a Materials Person.

5. The Materials Person does the following:

   • Obtains four sheets of copy paper. Places one sheet in front of each team member to form one large block.
   • Places one set of markers near the team.

6. The team brainstorms familiar nouns and selects one for the Captain to write on an index card. The noun may be a person, animal, event, object, or place.

7. The Captain places the noun card in the center of the four sheets of paper, or block.

Part II

1. Tell team members to number off to identify who will be responsible for each type of writing: descriptive, expository, persuasive, or narrative.

2. Each team member writes his or her type of writing at the top of the paper. Each member is responsible for recording the brainstormed ideas in an assigned graphic organizer on the sheet of copy paper.

Part III

The teacher gives directions for each student to create a graphic organizer for the type of writing, as outlined below. The group listens to the directions and observes as the team member draws the organizer. Students in each block party brainstorm information to assist each team member with ideas to complete the organizer. Encourage the team to use Figure 4.3 to focus on each type of writing.

Note: Each team member draws the organizer for his or her type of writing on the sheet of copy paper as the teacher provides directions. When each member's organizer has been drawn, other team members brainstorm ideas to complete each organizer.

Block 1   Descriptive Writing

1. Draw a circle to represent the sun.

2. Write the selected noun in the center of the circle.

3. Draw rays or lines extending from the circle. This creates a sunshine web. Place an attribute, a descriptive word or phrase, to describe the noun on each line.

Block 2   Expository Writing

1. On your sheet of paper, list words or phrases about the selected noun to use in a newspaper advertisement.

2. Write the list in graffiti style using colored markers or pens.

Block 3   Persuasive Writing

1. Draw the outline of your hand in the center of the paper or block.

2. Write the selected noun in the palm of the hand.

3. On each finger, tell why the noun is "the best."

Block 4   Narrative Writing

1. Fold your paper into six sections.

2. Write one of the following in each of the six sections: *Who?, What?, When?, Where?, Why?,* and *How?*

3. Respond to the question in each box by relating it to the selected noun. The writing in each box may be fiction or nonfiction.

Part IV

Find a comfortable place to write one or more paragraphs individually, using the type of writing identified in your block. You may use the ideas recorded on your organizer to complete the writing activity. However, you do not have to use all the ideas gathered during the prewriting activity, and you may add other thoughts while you are writing that are not on your organizer. Follow these directions for your type of writing:

Descriptive writing: Describe your noun for a special exhibit or event.

Expository writing: Write an ad for the noun to appear in the local newspaper.

Persuasive writing: Convince judges that your noun should win an award.

Narrative writing: Write one or more paragraphs about the noun by responding to the six questions.

Note to teachers: Remind the authors that they are using the group brainstorming as a *prewriting* activity. As they begin writing, they are creating their first draft or sloppy copy, the second step in the writing process.

Part V

1. Students return to their block party team.

2. They take turns sharing their writing with the block party group.

3. Each block party shares one type of writing.

4. They choose one example from their block party to share with the total group.

5. Celebrate!

Students place the block party writing in their portfolios as a later revision option.

THE WRITING PROCESS

Donald Graves's groundbreaking work *Writing: Teachers and Children at Work* (1983) describes writing as a process to be undertaken. Calkins (1994) and Atwell (1998) explain writing as a collaborative process among the student-author, the teacher, and other students. A writing process provides simple, sequential steps for the writer to use. The common titles for the steps are prewriting, drafting, revising, editing, final copy, and publishing. It is not necessary to take a student through all steps in the process in each writing activity. The purpose of a writing activity may be simply for the student to gather the information. In other words, one of the lesson objectives may be for the learner to use writing to stimulate thinking and reflection. In this case, the act of writing is the product. The authors may complete the first draft and share it.

Practice the Process

The following song, "I'm an Author," teaches the steps in the writing process. One verse can be used to introduce each step.

I'm an Author

(Sing to the tune "Are You Sleeping?")

Prewriting! Prewriting!

Gather thoughts, get data.

Pull my thoughts together.

This is my time to think.

Brainstorming! Brainstorming!

Drafting! Drafting!

Place your thoughts in order.

Write them down. Don't skip words.

This is my first draft.

Sloppy copy! Sloppy copy!

Revising! Revising!

Work on words. Reorganize.

Give it style. Add pizzazz!

Now my words will flow.

Ham it up! Ham it up!

Editing! Editing!

Check capitals and spelling.

Correct punctuation.

These are the mechanics.

Tune it up! Tune it up!

Final copy! Final copy!

Add changes. Write neatly.

Make it easy to read.

This is called a rewrite.

Neat sheet! Neat sheet!

Publishing! Publishing!

Display it! Share it now!

I'm a proud writer.

I'm a published author.

Celebrate! Celebrate!

—Chapman and King

Here are more activities to guide students in learning the sequenced steps in the writing process:

- Add explanations to the steps, as needed.
- Write the steps in graffiti style on banners, mobiles, and bulletin boards.
- Illustrate each step.
- Rap the steps to a catchy beat.
- Create a design with the name of each step.
- Write a cheer or a chant to use with each step.

Process the Process

Students need to know and understand the steps in the writing process. Teach the name of each step and refer to it often so the words become a part of the learners' vocabulary. Use the same terminology each time the step is used. Require students to use the appropriate terms when engaged in conversations and activities related to the writing process. They need opportunities to rehearse the words often and in many ways so they can automatically use them in their writing vocabulary.

One forgets words as one forgets names. One's vocabulary needs constant fertilizing or it will die.

—Evelyn Waugh, British author

STEP 1. GETTING STARTED: PREWRITING

The purpose of the prewriting session is for the author to prepare for writing. It is the step before the first draft of the product. If prewriting is used correctly, students are eager and prepared to write. These experiences are planned to create the students' desire to write about specific topics. The session hooks the learner on the activity, and the student gathers data and organizes thoughts related to the information. Effective prewriting activities create better first drafts. The information gathered becomes a reference tool for referral during the writing experience.

Teacher's Role for the Prewriting Step

Use a formal or informal preassessment tool to identify students' prior knowledge about a topic before planning lessons. Find out what they know and what they are interested in learning about the topic. Link the topic to the students' current and prior experiences. The connections stimulate their desire to learn more.

If the student has little or no experience with a writing topic, provide time for the author to create his or her background knowledge for the assignment. Whenever possible, let the student choose the writing topic. The learner usually selects familiar topics or personal interest areas with mental images needed for prewriting.

Introduce the Prewriting Assignment

Introduce the prewriting assignment to the student to answer such questions as "What is it?" "What is the purpose of this assignment?" "What will I be doing during this time?"and "Who will be in my audience?"

Set expectations with specific purposes for the writing experience. For example, let students know they need to brainstorm and gather ideas to use in the upcoming writing assignment. Share criteria to answer questions a student may unconsciously ask, such as "Why am I doing this?" "What is in this assignment for me?" or "Why should I complete this assignment?" Explain the criteria in clear, simple terms. Motivate the learner. Keep the assignment alive and exciting.

Identify the audience that will hear or read the writer's thoughts. The audience may be the author, a partner, a small group, or a large group. An audience may be real or imaginary. Teach the student to identify the audience and write as if talking directly to the person or group of people. Vary the audience to add novelty to the lessons.

Hook the learner during prewriting experiences. Hooks are motivating activities designed to intrigue, challenge, and focus the student's attention on the writing experience. Hooks can play on the senses. They build interest, evoke curiosity, and stir the imagination. A hook is effective when a student is eager to start writing.

Create an atmosphere of wonder through anticipation, surprise, and fascination in relation to the topic. Use curiosity to focus the learner's attention on the information and stimulate thinking. For example, if you assume the role of a soldier in the Civil War, the student will say, "I wonder what my teacher will think of next!"

Vary assignment strategies used to gather information. Provide opportunities for students to work with others and time to work alone in the prewriting stage. Strategically vary assignments throughout the plans so students apply different strategies to complete the tasks. Variety is the key!

Prewriting Strategies and Tools—Examples

- Brainstorm a word list related to the topic.
- Plot information on a graphic organizer.
- Complete a language experience activity.
- Design illustrations with labels and options.
- Compile a list.
- Categorize terms.
- Jigsaw the information.

- Read a selection.
- Engage in partner discussions.
- Gather ideas in small groups.
- Go on a scavenger hunt for information.
- Introduce a step-by-step procedure.
- Use a think, pair, share activity.
- Listen to music related to the topic.

Choose an Appropriate Graphic Organizer

Choose an appropriate graphic organizer that corresponds to the information the students will gather. For instance, if the study involves insects, use an outline of the critter. If the study is about space, use an outline of a rocket. The organizer categorizes and arranges the author's ideas, so concentration is on the flow of ideas related to the content. The first draft is easier to complete when ideas are gathered and recorded on an organizer.

Strategically Plan Prewriting Experiences

Figure 4.4 is a suggested checklist of ideas to use in preparing for prewriting.

Figure 4.4   Teacher's Prewriting Preparation: A Checklist
❑ 1. Select the topic or create a list of topic choices.
❑ 2. Analyze the preassessment to identify needs.
❑ 3. Identify your instructional grouping scenarios.
❑ 4. Choose an intriguing strategy or activity to hook students on the topic.
❑ 5. Identify an activity for reviewing or building the knowledge foundation.
❑ 6. Determine the length of the assignment.
❑ 7. Select the form or genre for the author to use or provide choices; for example, song, play, essay, or list.
❑ 8. Identify the reading or listening audience.
❑ 9. Establish the purpose of the writing assignment; for example, to share with a partner, to create test study notes, or to publish.
❑ 10. Select the type of paper to use; for example, unlined, textured, or a shape.
❑ 11. Choose the writing instruments; for example, pencil, pen, marker, or word processor.
❑ 12. Identify the length of time needed for the writing activity.
❑ 13. Select the formal or informal assessment tool for the writing assignment.

Prewriting Guidelines

After decisions and plans are made for the prewriting stage, use the guidelines in Figure 4.5 during the experience.

An Author's Self-Talk Guide for Prewriting

Teach students how to use self-talk to guide their prewriting experiences. Have students use statements similar to those in Figure 4.6 to analyze their prewriting preparation for the first draft.

Figure 4.5   Prewriting Guidelines

1. Set the tone for the writing experience.
2. Give clear, specific directions and guidelines.
3. Check for the learner's understanding of the assignment.
4. If choices are provided for writing genres or forms, provide time for student selection.
5. Give the authors time to collect and write their thoughts.
6. Ask open-ended questions to generate and extend thinking; for example, What would you do if _____?
7. Be a listener. Probe and jog the student's mind for ideas.
8. Encourage the student to pull the ideas together.
9. Build a spirit of helpfulness by encouraging students to share information and ideas.
10. Make materials and supplies accessible.
11. Check with the student to be sure the assignment and expectations are understood.
12. Show your enthusiasm!

Figure 4.6   Author's Self-Talk for Prewriting

- My assignment is _____.
- I need to _____.
- The topic of my writing will be _____.
- When I think about this subject, I already know _____.
- Before I write, I need to know _____.
- I could gather more information from _____. (For example: my notes, the text, the library, interviews, or the Internet)
- The best genre to use to share my ideas is _____.
- My reader or audience will be _____.
- My role as the author for this piece of writing is _____. (For example: a character, a bystander, a storyteller)
- I will need help with _____.
- My purpose for writing this selection is _____.
- The writing tools and materials I need are _____.
- The best place for me to write is _____.

Idea Roundup: Crucial Collections

The collection of data and ideas about a topic is crucial for prewriting. *Data* includes all information needed for the writing activity. The collection time is more important for some writing assignments than others.

Vary the gathering techniques. The student may know a lot about a topic from personal experiences but may need time to collect thoughts and write notes. The student uses notes to organize thoughts. Reports or informational essays require more data. As facts are collected, the student learns more about the subject.

Many avenues exist for students to search for information and ideas. Teach young authors how to use various collection tools. For example, give students opportunities to go on a scavenger hunt to gather information in the text, on the Internet, on a reference shelf, or through interviews. When they know how to use the strategies independently, encourage them to choose the most beneficial collection tool for the writing activity.

Provide time for writers to share the information as it is collected. The listening students can add new ideas and suggestions for the author.

Collection Selections

The following list contains suggested resources and ideas for collecting information:

books	magazines	movies	documentaries	Web searches
T.V. shows	news articles	brochures	brainstorming	plays
charts	drawings	organizers	quotations	observations
notes	experiments	interviews	journal notes	language
products	exhibits	imagination	drawings	experience

(See also the "Gathering Research" section in Chapter 5.)

STEP 2. SLOPPY COPY: FIRST DRAFT

Like butterflies freed from cages . . .

Thoughts fly from my mind, filling many pages.

—Chapman and King

The goal of this step of the writing process is to organize the thoughts gathered during the prewriting stage. The author writes the words freely, as though telling someone the information in story form. Tell students to draw a smiley face on a sticky note and place the note on their desks. Tell them to pretend they are talking to the smiley face and to write each word exactly as they say it. This approach creates organization and flow for the content of the writing passage.

This stage is referred to as the "sloppy copy" because the author does not stop to consider the correct spelling or mechanics. Students may experience "writer's block" when there is an emphasis on correct spelling and mechanics. ("Mechanics" include punctuation and capitalization.) This hampers the author's flow of ideas. Invented spelling is strongly recommended in the first draft. Tell the student to concentrate on the content and organization of the topic. Explain that spelling and other errors will be corrected in later stages of the writing process.

Remember, students who are struggling with the writing skills may have thoughts similar to the following:

The Struggling Writer's Wish

Wurdzs just floot a round en mi head. Whin I'm towld to rite thim on paepr, eye em affade, eye wont bee abell to splel the wurz kurrectlee. Eye haev greight eyedeeaas an the rite anserz to shair, but eye doughn't wont tu bee imbarasst and phill eshamed. Sinz eye kaent spel, eye no I kaent rite liek mi phrends. Sum da eye wil bee a famuz riter weth a sekreteri to rite 4 me!

When a writer expresses thoughts in first draft writing, accept the ideas with well-deserved praise. Remind students that some of the best authors have personal editors who convert their ideas into easy to understand, legible passages. Emphasize the value of ideas in each writing experience.

Teacher's Role in the First Draft

Create a positive, nonthreatening environment so students feel free to take risks. Learners need to hear the teacher's enthusiasm and excitement before drafting begins and as writing is shared. Tell students to find a comfortable spot to write their first draft. Use positive comments and words of encouragement. Expect success!

Model being a writer. Join students in personal writing when they are engaged in creating the first draft. This gives students opportunities to observe someone modeling the first draft experience. It is amazing to see how everyone stays on-task when the teacher writes.

Believe students can write. Lead students in repeating, "If I can say it, I can write it!" They need to understand that writing is the author's "talk written down." Share the following statements as a strategy to keep students focused on placing their thoughts on paper: "Pretend you are telling this information to someone standing beside you or draw a face on a sticky note. Talk to that person and write each word exactly as you say it. Do not skip a word or thought." When writers learn to use this strategy, believe in their own ability, and use it, they become better writers.

Explain the purpose and value of first draft writing, making students aware of its importance. For example, first draft writing prepares students to respond to open-ended questions on tests; in most assessments, they are not permitted to correct their writing. First draft writing is used to complete many assignments. It is also the way most people write in their daily activities.

Avoid taking all writing through the entire publishing process. When students know how to complete first drafts, they are on the path to becoming successful authors.

Encourage invented spelling. Invented spelling uses the sounds of letters to spell. This phonetic spelling enhances creative writing. When invented spelling is accepted, the student has more freedom to record thoughts without concern for correctness. Emphasis on correct spelling interferes with the learner's concentration on content and organization during first draft writing.

Always ask the author to read his or her own first draft writing, because invented spelling is easily misinterpreted. For example, if the student writes, "ilikmihos," it could be interpreted as "I like my house," or "I like my horse." When phonetic spelling is accepted, the student uses more words with multiple syllables. For example, *klorafil* may be written for *chlorophyll* and *fotosinthesis* for *photosynthesis*. The author can pronounce the word while reading his or her own writing to describe the color-changing process of leaves. Remember, a student's speaking and writing vocabulary is usually much larger than the spelling vocabulary.

The first draft emphasizes the importance of focusing on recording content ideas and organization. Spelling corrections are made later in the editing stage of the writing process, after thoughts are placed on paper. The words a student spells correctly in the first draft are the mastered words. The learner spells these words automatically. This means that first draft writing can be used as an assessment tool to identify mastered spelling words, grammar, and punctuation.

It may be difficult to make decisions related to spelling expectations during writing activities. Language arts specialists have debated spelling requirements in writing activities for many years. The latest research overwhelmingly supports invented spelling in first draft writing. Students become more creative with their writing ideas when invented spelling is accepted.

Spelling Guidelines for Writing Activities

The following research-based suggestions related to invented spelling are presented to assist teachers in applying spelling guidelines to writing activities:

- The first draft is the "sloppy copy." The emphasis is not on correct spelling during first draft writing. Rather, during this step in the writing process, the author focuses attention on the content and organization of the information.

- Prewriting samples are not graded. They can, however, be used as assessments of spelling and mechanical skills. For example, if a student uses periods correctly while writing the first draft, he or she has reached the level of automaticity with the skill.

- Spelling corrections are made while editing the work. Use a response similar to the following when a student asks for the spelling of a word during the first draft session: "Listen to the sounds in the word and then spell it your way." The student needs assurance that misspelled words are accepted. Remind the author not to omit, substitute, or use a smaller word because the selected word is difficult to spell. Model this technique several times, because students may not be accustomed to leaving mistakes in their work. Routinely remind the class that ideas are more important than correct spelling in the first writing stages.

- More first drafts are completed than later steps in the writing process. If the writer is asked to go through every step of the process with each paper, the desire to write may be inhibited. Every paper does not need to go through several revisions. The student needs more sloppy copies than "neat sheets," because an author learns to write by writing!

Remember, phonics is taught more widely today than in the past decade. In the future, the student will have more background knowledge to use invented spelling. More programs will be accessible.

Figure 4.7 shows the readiness level of specific groups in the classroom. The preassessment data identify the information the students at these three levels need to learn. The learners at each level of mastery are in a category because of their individual knowledge base—that is, their personal experience and background with a particular topic, skill, or standard.

Figure 4.7 Adjustable Assignment for Invented Spelling		
B	• Give specific praise. • Encourage spelling of multisyllable words. • Provide opportunities to read own writing.	• Build confidence and security. • Reassure that incorrect spelling will not be graded. • Praise independent attempts to tackle unfamiliar words.	• Model the strategies. • Teach the strategies and techniques for invented spelling. • Articulate aloud the step-by-step thinking needed to spell words phonetically. • Provide more phonics background. • Teach rules and how to apply them.
A	• Is eager to express ideas in writing. • Is secure and confident in make spelling attempts. • Has a strong phonics background. • Understands that invented spelling enhances flow of thought. • Knows how to use invented spelling automatically in the first draft.	• Tries to spell words independently. • Has some phonics background. • Uses invented spelling occasionally. • Feels insecure with the process. • Asks for assistance when spelling difficult words.	• Does not have a strong phonics background. • Does not understand invented spelling techniques. • "Shuts down." • Does not write the big words he is thinking and saying. • Asks for assistance.
	High Degree of Mastery	*Approaching Mastery*	*Beginning Mastery*

Standard: To be able to use invented spelling

Key:

A. What do they know now?

B. What do they need to learn next?

The Drafting Craft: Guidelines for Students

Figure 4.8 offers students a checklist to guide their drafting process.

Figure 4.8   Guidelines for the Drafting Craft

To create my first draft, I need to do the following:

- ☐ 1. Find a comfortable place to think and write.
- ☐ 2. Skip lines for revising and editing.
- ☐ 3. Use my prewriting brainstorming notes, ideas, and organizers.
- ☐ 4. Pretend I am telling the story to someone.
- ☐ 5. Write every word without skipping or omitting anything.
- ☐ 6. Include new ideas on the topic that come to me as I write.
- ☐ 7. Use capitalization and punctuation marks as needed.
- ☐ 8. Spell words the way they sound, if I don't know how to spell them.
- ☐ 9. Read the first draft to myself and make corrections.
- ☐ 10. Read my completed first draft to a peer, a small group, or the teacher.

Off to a Smart Start: Beginning the First Draft

Share examples and ideas for first draft writing. Discuss the value and purpose of having a strong introduction to the first draft and for using strategies for effective writing throughout the introduction, development, and conclusion of the draft.

Teach the following strategies as needed to guide students through first draft writing experiences:

Introduction

- Grab the reader's attention in the first few lines.
- Choose a unique, quality beginning to entice your reader to keep reading.
- Ask profound questions to build curiosity.
- Tell your idea or story from a unique point of view.

Development

- Stay with your topic or main idea.
- Use fascinating facts and supporting details.
- Add style with similes, idioms, metaphors, and analogies.
- Add detail with questions, verbs, adjectives, and adverbs.
- Compare or contrast your information with a familiar event, person, or object.
- Engage the reader's emotions and senses.
- Use detailed descriptions to establish the plot, describe the scene, and create the characters.

Conclusion

- Restate the purpose of the passage in the summary or closing.
- Read the passage to yourself to decide if the piece needs more or less information.
- Refine the work and then read it to a peer or adult, or read it to yourself again, if a listener is not available.

Publishing Drafts

When first drafts are displayed, announce that the work has not been revised or edited. Inform sloppy copy audiences that writing style, content, and organization have been emphasized and that punctuation, capitalization, and other writing mechanics are not the major focus in this step of the work.

Display Spaces for Drafts

journals	clotheslines	walls	ribbons
ropes	charts	transparency sleeves	
stations	bulletin boards	writing folders	

Signs for Draft Displays

First Draft Writing	Writing under Construction
Draft Craft	Work in Progress
Sloppy Copies	

Clearing Away the Cobwebs

New ideas are easier to weave into writing when thoughts are clear, so it may be necessary to remove mental cobwebs. Students need to understand the value of putting their work out of sight for a time. The time away from writing often provides a needed mental escape and clears cobwebs from their minds. New, fresh ideas are more likely to come when they return to the writing. Provide students with handy storage places to keep their writing as the cobwebs clear.

Conferencing Guidelines for Reviewing First Drafts

The following are suggested steps for students to use during first draft conferences:

1. Raise your hand when you complete your first draft.
2. Wait for the teacher to assign you a partner.
3. Choose a comfortable place to work together.
4. Take a pencil so you can make revisions during your first reading.
5. Read your writing aloud to your partner. As you read, correct obvious errors, including omitted words, extra words, capitalization, and punctuation.

6. Discuss the selection with your partner.

7. Take notes on your partner's suggestions to consider for correction and improvement.

8. Now it is time to hear the listening partner's first draft.

STEP 3. HAMMING IT UP: REVISION

I rewrote the ending to Farewell to Arms, *the last page of it, thirty-nine times, before I was satisfied.*

—Ernest Hemingway

The revision step in the writing process is designed for the author to organize the content, make additions, and delete unnecessary information. The writer checks the flow of ideas and the organization, conveyance, and intent of the message. As the author reads, the listener needs to understand the message. Style is added in this step. The author evaluates the work and makes corrections to move the writing toward excellence.

Teacher's Role in Revision

Assign Revisions Selectively

Remember, it is not necessary to take all writing assignments through the revision process. Students need to practice getting their ideas on paper many times, so they need to complete prewriting and drafting steps often. Students are more motivated to write when they are not required to revise each assignment.

Allow the Student to Select a Piece of Work to Revise

Each student does not have to revise the same writing piece. For best results, ask the author to choose a first draft selection from the topic folder or notebook. The author will be more interested in making revisions on a chosen piece. Also, the author usually demonstrates the best work when he or she knows the writing will appear in a display or publication.

Make Revisions to the First Draft

Revisions are easier to make when lines are skipped in the first draft. Show the writer how to use arrows, carets (^), and other symbols to indicate places to add and delete words or phrases. Many students enjoy using scissors or a word processing program to cut and paste phrases, sentences, and paragraphs when revising because these tasks are easier than rewriting.

Plan Revision Conferences

Revision conferences take place with the author reading the work to a partner, a small group, or the teacher. Revision is primarily the student's responsibility; the author may include suggestions of others but makes the final revision decisions. The revision process is time consuming, but the writer needs to participate in dialogues about possible changes. Conferences provide opportunities for the author to generate improvement ideas. Make this time a pleasant experience for everyone involved. The goal of the conference is to move the student's writing toward excellence.

Identify the Number of Changes According to the Student's Needs

The writer may decide he or she is not capable of writing, if too many revisions are cited. The writer who steeps in frustration or anger is turned off to writing experiences. Be aware of negative attitudes. Avoid requirements for the author to correct every mistake. Each improvement to the writing is an indicator that the student is growing as an author. Remind students that revisions are designed to improve writing, not to perfect it. In revision conferences, the author maintains control of corrections. If someone revises too much of the work, the author may no longer feel in control of the writing.

Make Revision a Step in Learning for the Author

Revision suggestions may come from the author or other individuals. The writer approves of each change and correction. If the author and editor disagree, the author makes the final decisions about the suggested changes. The student learns writing skills by considering ideas for revision and making corrections.

Putting Style in Writing

Writing style is the way the individual writer states ideas on paper. This style sets the writer apart from other writers. Each author has unique ideas and style. For example, one writer may use many words and details for expression, while another may use a few words and less detail. Each approach reflects the author's individual style.

Style makes writing unique! Just as a person dresses with individual style, the author's originality and personality are reflected in the writing. The following guidelines are designed for a student to learn while implementing personal style in each writing selection.

Add Adjectives

Teach students how to add adjectives to describe the characters and the setting. Give them the following suggested guidelines to add the special describing words. Also, make an ongoing class list of adjectives on a visible chart.

1. Find important nouns in the first draft.

2. Place a caret (^) in front of each noun to hold a place for one or more adjectives.

3. Add an adjective or adjectives above the carets to describe each noun.

4. Read the sentence, the old version and the new one, to your partner.

5. Ask your partner to give a thumbs-up if the phase is improved with the new adjective. Ask for a thumbs-down if the adjective did not improve the phrase.

6. Decide if the changes are needed. Remember, as the author, you make the final decisions about the changes.

7. Make needed changes on your sloppy copy.

Add Adverbs

Teach students how to add adverbs to verbs, making the character, scenes, or events easier to visualize. Use the following suggested guidelines with students to add adverbs to their writing. Also, make an ongoing class list of adverbs on a visible chart.

1. Find important verbs in the first draft.

2. Place a caret (^) before or after the verb.

3. Add an adverb to describe the verb.

4. Read the original phrase and the phrase with the new word to your partner. Ask your partner to give a thumbs-up if the phrase is improved with the new adverb. Ask your partner to give a thumbs-down if the adverb does not improve the phrase.

5. As the author, you decide if the change is needed.

6. Make your changes on the sloppy copy.

Add WOW Words!

"WOW words" are words and phrases that end with an exclamation point. They express strong feelings and emotions, from frustration to excitement. Make a chart of "WOW words" for the classroom. Have students generate words that require an exclamation point. Remind writers to add exclamations to dialogue. Find places in the writing to add WOW words on the sloppy copy.

Examples

Awesome!	Crash!	Bang!	Help!	Oh, no!	Oh, yes!
Uh-oh!	Yeah!	Yes!	Yikes!	Wow!	Help!

Add Dialogue or Conversation

Dialogue evokes emotion and places the reader in the scene with the characters. When writing dialogue, avoid overuse of words. For instance, substitute words for *said* to show the characters' true feelings in conversations.

Instead of Said: Activity

1. Teach students how to replace *said* with other action verbs. Create a class list of words to substitute for *said.* Tell the student to copy the list and place it in the writing folder as a reference tool.

Examples

cried	laughed	whimpered	wept
squealed	yelled	whispered	yelped
griped	complained	confessed	giggled

2. Tell the student to look through a writing selection and draw a line through the word *said*. Ask the learner to write a word that reflects the character's emotion above the word *said*.

Said in Your Head: Activity

1. Create cards with words that can substitute for *said*.

2. Assign partners.

3. Each partner team draws a replacement word for *said*.

4. Partners select actions to role-play the word and practice.

5. Form a class circle.

6. Call on each partner team to display their word and role-play actions to describe the word.

7. Ask classmates to guess each word.

Vary the Type of Sentences

Teach the learner to write sentences in an inviting order so readers clearly understand the meaning of the text. Take the boredom out of a passage by varying the type of sentences.

- Use WOW words to add excitement and feelings to writing. Exclamatory sentences create emotions; for example, Wow! Zing! What pizzazz!.

- Use statements to tell or explain. Declarative sentences tell readers what you want them to know.

- Ask questions. Questions create curiosity. They may indicate that an exciting answer will follow. Interrogative sentences make the reader think of a response or guess what comes next.

- Give a command, a direction, or an order. Use imperative sentences to call for an action.

Use Figurative Language

Teach students how to add flair and style by using figurative language, such as similes, metaphors, and analogies.

- *Similes* compare two unlike things using the words *like* or *as*. Following are some examples:

  She was as pretty as a rose in springtime.

  He was strong, like a bulldozer.

- *Metaphors* compare two things or concepts without using the words *like* or *as*. Metaphors equate the two ideas in some way. Here is an example:

  Learning is a lifelong journey.

- An analogy is used to explain the similarity of two people or things. A common format used for analogies is this: _____is to _____ as _____is to _____. Here are two examples:

  January is to winter as October is to fall.

  Drop is to rain as flake is to snow.

Using the Mind's Eye

Teach the writer to be conscious of the visual pictures or images in his or her mind. A student cannot produce mental pictures without experiences to create them. For example, if an author writes about Egyptian pyramids, prior knowledge must exist to produce the images.

The writer's level of knowledge varies according to prior experiences. The student with a strong knowledge base on the subject has more descriptors for writing. Provide the learner with many opportunities to use describing words. Have the writer draw a picture first, then write about it. The illustration creates a concrete visual to use as a handy writing tool. Practice the use of describing words by selecting familiar writing topics, such as a tree changing the color of its leaves.

Digging Deeper for Details

When a student writes an inadequate amount of information, more details are needed. The learner needs to dig deeper into the main idea or topic. For example, if the author has one or two stand-alone sentences, the idea needs elaboration or embellishment. Try the following strategy to teach the student how to add needed detail to a passage:

1. Ask the author to read the sentences aloud.

2. Say, "Tell me more about _____." Remember, it is easier for students to "tell it" than to "write it."

3. Ask the student to write exactly the words he or she said without skipping a word. The listener takes notes and leaves them with the author so they can be used as a reference when writing resumes.

4. Guide the student to realize that writing is simply "talk written down" for someone to read or for the author to use later.

Key Marks for Revision

Use the following key as a handy tool to use for revisions. Teach the author how to use the key for self-monitoring or to prepare for a revision conference.

? I need to go back to this section for more work.

! This part is on target.

× This section may need to be deleted.

+ I need to add more information here.

Revision Conferences: Sharing the Work

Schedule a conference at this point in the writing process. The author reads the work orally to a partner, a small group, or the teacher. The listeners give the author specific suggestions for improvements at the end of the reading session.

Sharing the Writing

The work is shared so the author hears the work and has someone's listening ear to provide feedback. The author reads his or her own writing to the audience.

When suggestions are accepted, the student internalizes skills while actively applying them. This experience develops critical thinking and interpersonal skills. The author needs to know the revision conference is designed to strengthen the writing sample. The student can use the following guidelines for sharing work.

Guidelines for Partner Revisions

1. Choose a writing sample.
2. Take your writing sample and pencil to meet your partner.
3. Find a cozy place to work.
4. Read the selection to the listening partner.
5. As you read, make changes on your sloppy copy. For example, fill in omitted words or mark out unnecessary words.
6. The listener makes positive comments with specific suggestions.
7. Take turns sharing ideas to improve the writing.
8. The partners discuss each revision, but the author makes the final decision about changing the work.

Variation: The guidelines can be used for group revisions.

Teach students how to give suggestions to the writer in ways that improve the piece and maintain the author's feeling of ownership. Teach and reinforce the rules for productive sharing. Discuss and practice appropriate ways to make suggestions. Here are some examples.

Listener's Guidelines for Revisions

- Respect the author and the selection.
- Listen carefully.
- Ask specific questions.
- Make positive comments.
- Give constructive suggestions for making the paper better.

Here are a few examples of the guidelines in action:

- I like _____ because _____.
- What is your favorite part?
- What do you think would make your writing better?
- How can I help you?

Use specific prompts such as the following to work constructively with partners:

Listener Discussion Prompts for Revisions

- You could _____.
- Try adding _____.
- This sentence would sound better if _____.
- Try saying it this way: _____.
- Let's try _____.
- Read it without _____.
- Tell me more about _____.
- Explain the section _____.
- Let's move _____ to _____.

Author's Discussion Prompts for Revisions

- What did you like about my writing?
- What would make this passage better?
- Do I need to leave out or add words, phrases, or sentences?
- Do I need to substitute a better word or phrase?
- Do I need to move a section?
- Do you have other suggestions for improving my work?

Reflection and Revising the Work

The author takes notes, sample work, and conference suggestions to a quiet spot and makes revisions on the sloppy copy. When all revisions are complete, the revision checklist in Figure 4.9 can be used as a reflection guide. It identifies areas that need more work in the writing or indicates that the work is complete. Provide the author with a self-evaluation checklist similar to the one in Figure 4.10 before or after the conference or revisions.

Figure 4.9   Author's Revision Checklist

- ☐ 1. I wrote what I was thinking.
- ☐ 2. The beginning is interesting and hooks the reader.
- ☐ 3. I included important, accurate information.
- ☐ 4. I tapped into the reader's senses with my descriptions.
- ☐ 5. All sentences are clear, correct, and in order.
- ☐ 6. I replaced simple words with more interesting words.
- ☐ 7. The sentences have varied beginnings, lengths, and styles.
- ☐ 8. The details support the main idea.
- ☐ 9. I used different types of sentences, such as declarative, interrogatory, exclamatory, and imperative.
- ☐ 10. I added needed words, phrases, or sentences.
- ☐ 11. I deleted words, phrases, or sentences that need to be removed.
- ☐ 12. I moved parts of the passage that needed to move.
- ☐ 13. I have an interesting closing.
- ☐ 14. I am proud of my work!

Figure 4.10   Author's Self-Evaluation Checklist

- ☐ 1. I have enough information.
- ☐ 2. My work is interesting and easy to read.
- ☐ 3. The information is accurate.
- ☐ 4. My report is informative.
- ☐ 5. My writing sends the message I want to convey.
- ☐ 6. I considered all suggestions.
- ☐ 7. I used correct sources.
- ☐ 8. My paragraphs are in order.
- ☐ 9. My introduction grabs the reader's attention.
- ☐ 10. I have a quality conclusion.
- ☐ 11. My paper is written neatly so it can be read easily.
- ☐ 12. My work is written in my own words.

Out With the Old, In With the New: Writing Habits

Habits are hard to break. Students must have a strong desire, or buy-in, to break a writing habit. They must be convinced that the new skill or strategy is better than the one they currently use.

Identify ineffective writing habits to make the author aware of specific problems. Modeling is an excellent way to demonstrate correct writing. Remember, it takes time, practice, and patience to change a poor writing habit.

Habits to Break

- Uses too many words to express thoughts.

  Do not say the same thing twice. Identify unnecessary words.

  If you need to explain or repeat something, use different words.

- Uses too few words.

  Use enough words to make your points and create understanding.

- Uses "big words."

  Big words are not always the best choice.

  Use the best words, not necessarily the biggest words.

- Uses too many *I* words.

  Use other pronouns or rephrase the sentence.

- Writes unnecessary information.

  Write about topics or subjects that are of interest or needed by readers. Remember, "If the information is interesting or needed, they will read it!"

I can't understand how anyone can write without rewriting everything over and over again. I scarcely ever re-read my published writings, but if by chance I come across a page, it always strikes me: All this must be rewritten; this is how I should have written it.

—Leo Tolstoy

STEP 4. TUNING IT UP: EDITING

The editing step in the writing process provides time for the author to correct spelling, punctuation, capitalization, grammar, and the overall appearance of the selection. Remind the author to take the writing, the revisions, and a pencil when meeting with the partner or small group. The author reads the writing. The editing goal is for the writer to improve the work by using the suggestions of others as a step in learning how to self-edit.

Teacher's Role for the Editing Step
Model

Model thinking and reasoning by demonstrating and explaining each procedure in the editing process. As the steps are introduced, sequentially and thoroughly, students learn the how-tos of editing.

Avoid Red Marks and Negative Comments

Let students mark errors on their own papers. Give them specific rules and guidelines. This is a learning process. Young authors learn through self-correction. Remind students that everyone learns from mistakes.

Give Students the Opportunity to Edit Their Own Work

Allow time for the students to work on their papers at the beginning of the editing stage. For example, they need to locate each misspelled word, circle it, look it up, and write the correct spelling above it.

Plan Partner or Small-Group Editing Conferences

In a conference, the audience offers suggestions as the author makes desired corrections. For example, the group may check the correct use of punctuation marks at the end of each sentence. This "punctuation talk" is an excellent way for students to share and learn writing skills.

Mechanics Antics

The mechanics of writing are the signs and symbols, such as punctuation and capitalization, placed in the writing. The signs and symbols guide readers' understanding of the author's expressions and meaning. When overemphasized, the placement of these signals often becomes a barrier to good writing. Used appropriately, however, these writing tools make the author's thoughts clear so the audience understands the ideas.

Sentence Sense

Each sentence must express a complete thought. Give the authors an opportunity to look for fragments and correct them. Be sure each sentence has a subject and verb.

Grammar Gab

The following "fix-it solutions" are included in the editing step of the writing process because this step involves choosing the right verb tenses, pairing nouns with the appropriate verbs, and pairing pronouns correctly with antecedents. Authors often recognize grammatical errors when they read their own work orally. Some common points to use in Grammar Gab follow:

- Sequence of tenses

  Wrong: He plays ball, studies his homework, and needed to go to work.

  Correct: He plays ball, studies his homework, and needs to go to work.

- Noun agreement

  Wrong: Jim and Jacob looks at the cows.

  Correct: Jim and Jacob look at the cows.

- Pronoun reference

  Wrong: The student works on the writing and then they meet with a partner to share the work.

  Correct: The student works on the writing, and then he meets with a partner to share the work.

Capitalization

Use a capital letter for the following:

- The first word in a sentence
- Names of people and special places
- Names of days of the week, months, and holidays
- Commercial products
- Names of organizations and groups
- Titles of books, movies, songs, poems, and articles
- Headings and subheadings

Sentence Stop Signs

- Use a period at the end of a declarative sentence. A declarative sentence "tells."
- Place a question mark at the end of an interrogative sentence. An interrogative sentence asks a question.
- Place an exclamation point at the end of an exclamatory sentence. An exclamatory sentence shows excitement.
- Place a period at the end of an imperative sentence. An imperative sentence gives a command or order.
- Be aware of a pause or "drop" in your writing voice because it usually indicates the need for a punctuation mark.

Comma Cues

Commas make the author's thoughts easy to read and understand. Here are some of the most common places to use a comma:

- Between the day and year in a date
- Between the city and state in an address

- Between two complete thoughts in a sentence that are connected with words such as *and, but, for, or, nor, so,* or *yet*
- On both sides of a proper noun when it is used in apposition; for example,"My dog, Abby, is a wonderful pet."
- After the greeting and closing comments in a letter
- Between words in a sequence
- To set off words in an introduction; for example,"First, . . . "

Colons: Dot Duo

A colon is used in the following situations:

- Before a list

  Find the following animals in your text: beaver, porcupine, squirrel, and bear.

- Before a long quotation in a passage

  Shakespeare reminds us: "To be or not to be . . ."

- After a formal greeting in a business letter

  To whom it may concern:

- Between the hour and minutes in a time

  School dismisses classes at 3:25 PM today.

Quotation Quotes

Use quotation marks to show what a person is saying. The marks go before and after a direct quote. Remember, it is not necessary to use quotation marks in a speech bubble when drawing cartoons. A speech bubble indicates that the individual near the bubble is talking without needing quotation marks as well.

Spelling Corrections

Ask the author to read the work to find spelling errors. Tell the writer to circle words spelled incorrectly and correct them on the sloppy copy. Encourage the author to use all available resources, such as a dictionary, thesaurus, spellcheck, textbook, word banks, and favorite cool tools (see "Razzmatazz to Thingamajigs" in Chapter 2). Partners can work together to find the correct spellings.

Tell students to create a personal dictionary of the new words so they won't have to look them up again. They may keep the list in a folder or journal.

Developing Spellers

Provide opportunities for students to work and/or play with a word that is difficult to spell. Use the students' intelligence strengths and learning styles in the activity to teach them the correct spelling of a word. For instance, if a student's strong areas of intelligence are art and music, create activities that spell words using colors; graffiti writing; or raps, jingles, or songs. If the speller enjoys working with others, assign a peer tutor or assistant to participate in spelling practice sessions and games.

Encourage the student to use the approach that works best to spell the word. The following list provides examples of some ways a student may learn to spell. (See also the discussion of invented spelling above under "Step 2. Sloppy Copy: First Draft.")

- Say the word and spell it with your finger in the air or in the palm of your hand.
- Color-code each syllable.
- Identify word families and rhyming words.
- Draw around the word to outline its shape. This shows the word's configuration.
- Draw a box around the root or base word.
- Circle the prefix and/or suffix.

Provide opportunities for the student to practice spelling words in varied ways. Practice the spelling of a word until the student takes ownership of the word, spelling it automatically.

Making Repairs

Use writing samples with incorrect punctuation, spelling mistakes, or grammatical errors to demonstrate ways to correct mechanical errors. Provide the student with shortcuts to correcting errors, such as cutting and pasting, drawing lines through them, and marking each one with an arrow. Use these activities when the student works alone, with a partner, with groups, or with the total class. Give students a checklist similar to Figure 4.11 to assist in the correction of mechanical errors.

Figure 4.11   Mechanical Checkup

Student _____ Date _____ Title _____

Skills	Yes	No	Comments
Each sentence begins with a capital letter.			
The names of people are capitalized.			
The names of special places and things begin with a capital letter.			
Correct punctuation is used at the end of my sentences.			
I corrected misspelled words.			
Someone read my work to be sure it made sense.			
I used quotation marks for dialogue.			
Paragraphs are indented.			
My words are spaced for easy reading.			
Others			

STEP 5. NEAT SHEET: FINAL COPY

After the editing step is complete, the work is ready to become a "neat sheet." The goal for the neat sheet is improvement, not perfection. The author uses the sloppy copy with the revision and editing notes to make the final copy. Design this final draft experience as an exciting, rewarding event to give the author a feeling of accomplishment and pride. Remind the student that the writing has progressed from his or her original thoughts through the steps of the writing process to produce the masterpiece. Remind the author that the final copy may contain errors but it reflects the writer's best work at this time.

The steps in the writing process take an author's work from the prewriting to the final copy. In most assignments, the student needs to work through the sloppy copy step, while very few writing assignments need to become neat sheets.

Teacher's Role in the Final Copy

Model Appearance Expectations for the Final Copy

Show tips and techniques for indenting, spacing, neatness, and legible writing. Remember, many genres use different formats. Share various formatting examples so the student can adapt the ideas in writing experiences. Refer to the writer as the "artist at work." Tell the author that the goal for the final copy is to produce the "best work" or "masterpiece."

Provide Time, Materials, and Space to Write the Neat Sheet

Consider individual needs for this step. Remind the author to use the revision and editing notes with the sloppy copy to develop the final edition. Provide quality writing implements and the appropriate paper. If a computer with writing software is available, allow the student to compose the final copy using a word processing program. Remember, a student may need extra time to complete this step in the writing process. If possible, let the student choose the "write spot" to work alone and concentrate.

Remember, the Goal Is to Improve Writing, Not to Perfect It

Compare the student's prewriting, sloppy copy, and final copy. Look for improvements. Assess strengths and weaknesses. The writer's growth through the experiences will be evident. Identify skills to teach or reinforce in future writing activities.

STEP 6. SHARING AND CELEBRATING: PUBLISHING

The author's work can be published at the end of any step in the writing process. The student could share the writing with teachers, classmates, or special guests in large or small groups. Sharing may involve formal or informal viewing of the work. Choose writing selections to place in a notebook, display on walls, post on the Web, or place in the student's portfolio. The publication is a presentation showcase of the author's "best work." It is time to celebrate!

Teacher's Role in Sharing and Celebrating
Provide Time for the Student to Share the Writing

Allow the reading of the selection with partners, small groups, and the total class. Invite an audience for the celebration, such as other classes, administrators, or honored guests. Give the author time to rehearse the reading before sharing with an audience. Watch the writer's confidence grow through these experiences.

Display the Author's Work

The student's work creates a print-rich environment related to the lesson. The writing samples make excellent bulletin board, wall, door, and hall displays. Take advantage of publishing opportunities for the young author in magazines, Web sites, newspapers, contests, and community displays.

Plan Reflection Periods for Students to Process the Experience

Students benefit from reflecting on their writing experiences in a journal. Encourage authors to think about the skills and strategies they learn along the way. Journaling provides opportunities for authors to express and analyze their feelings about writing. Each successful accomplishment creates positive attitudes toward the skill. If the reflection is negative, make changes. Information gained from reflective activities benefits the student and the teacher.

Be an Active Listener as the Author Reads

Give specific feedback for the selection read so the author realizes the value of having a good listener. If appropriate, provide the audience opportunities to enter the feedback discussion.

Express Interest and Enthusiasm for the Publication

Let students hear sincere, specific praise for their writing. Positive oral and written comments motivate writers. Praise, praise, praise! Praise the work to teachers, staff members, and parents in the student's presence. This recognition inspires and rewards young authors.

Publishing Debuts

Try some of the following suggestions for celebrating the authors' work and growth as writers. Ask students for more celebration ideas.

Authors' Reception

- Invite parents, grandparents, and special friends.
- Have a selection or book signing.
- Provide a cake decorated like a large book. Use balloons and confetti.

- Display the written masterpieces.
- Make banners to reflect words of celebration and congratulations.
- Ask the young authors to dress for the occasion.
- Designate an author's chair. (See the following "Author's Chair" section for guidelines.)
- Designate a master of ceremony to introduce the authors.
- Record or videotape the authors as they read.
- Present copies of the writing to the special guests.

Author's Chair

Designate an author's chair for the student to use when sharing with the total class. Use the following ideas to make the author's chair as a special event in the classroom or with invited guests:

1. Rehearse the first reading with partners or small groups to practice volume level, pauses, expressions, and mechanics.

2. Send an invitation to another class, parents, or special guests.

3. Designate a special area for the "Author's Chair" for the student's special reading. Place a reading lamp nearby. Use a podium and a microphone to make the event a more formal affair.

4. Have the author sign copies of his or her work.

More Publishing Ideas

- Create a video of the reading.
- Make a "big book" or a "mini book."
- Record the reading so others can listen to it. Use a distinctive sound before a page is turned.
- Add copies of the books of student writing to the class or school library.
- Enter writing selections in local, district, state, national, and international contests.
- Submit the writing to magazines for publication.
- Display student writing in the following places and spaces:

doors	hallways	parent letters	fliers	bulletin boards
newspapers	Web sites	store windows	magazines	clotheslines
handmade books	walls	cabinet doors	window shades	borders

Reflecting on Writing

Give students a checklist such as the one in Figure 4.12 to reflect on their writing.

Figure 4.12   Author's Reflections

Author _____ Date _____ Title _____

Think about the steps in the writing process and check the items you completed well.

☐   1. I brainstormed ideas.

☐   2. I discussed my ideas with a classmate.

☐   3. I used my time wisely to gather information.

☐   4. The details supported the main idea.

☐   5. The events were told in sequence.

☐   6. I included needed graphics in my writing.

☐   7. I read my work aloud to someone.

☐   8. I revised my work.

☐   9. I corrected mechanics: punctuation, capitalization, and spelling.

☐ 10. I am ready to publish my work.

Complete the following:

1. The hardest part of the writing experience was _____.

2. The easiest part of the writing experience was _____.

3. I still need to work on _____.

4. I improved my writing by _____.

Comments:

FLEXIBLE GROUPING

In the differentiated classroom, flexible groupings are essential to meeting the diverse needs of learners and writers. In planning content-related writing experiences, the teacher assesses the students' learning styles and preferences. The most effective grouping design is selected to meet the personal needs of each student. Consider the following questions:

- What arrangement will best allow the student to meet physical, social, and emotional needs?

- How does the student need to work to accomplish the task and reach his or her potential?

Use a variety of grouping designs. For example, use total groups when all students need to hear the same information. Such lessons include a prewriting activity, giving directions, or teaching an important writing skill.

In addition, students need time to process information and write what they are thinking independently. Give each learner opportunities to become a self-directed, confident writer.

Learning may be enhanced with partner work. Think of the active involvement that takes place when half of the class is engaged in talking or writing as the other half actively listens or observes. Partner and small-group assignments promote discussion, teaming, and sharing.

The author needs to be an active participant in a variety of working scenarios. The appropriate grouping for each writing opportunity makes the difference in the success of the activity.

TAPS

Writing activities are completed working with the **T**otal group (T), **A**lone (A), with a **P**artner (P), or with a **S**mall group (S). The TAPS acronym, designed by Gregory and Chapman (2006), sends the message for teachers to select the most effective grouping design that TAPS into each student's potential for a particular learning scene. Remember to plan writing groups according to the students' learning styles, intelligences, and writing personality (see Chapter 2). Keep in mind that students who are are socially compatible will work cooperatively to complete tasks.

Figure 4.13 lists suggested designs for specific writing activities. Some activities can be adapted to more than one design.

Figure 4.13	Flexible Grouping in the Differentiated Writing Classroom	
Group Designs	*Writing Tasks*	
Total Group	• Brainstorming lists • Creating graffiti fact boards • Responding to learning • Compiling rules • Reporting • Writing directions • Sharing information	• Gathering information • Making time lines • Completing direction charts • Plotting on a graphic organizer • Taking notes • Guided practice • Writing facts graffiti style
Alone	• Brainstorming • Solving a problem • Gathering research data • Recording in journals • Plotting on a graphic organizer • Completing independent work • Processing reflections • Working in a center	• Taking tests • Taking notes • Responding to learning • Answering questions • Answering open-ended questions • Recording in logs and diaries • Completing homework • Journaling
Partner	• Brainstorming • Peer-to-peer tutoring • Recording data • Plotting on a graphic organizer • Researching • Peer evaluations	• Conferencing with portfolios • Responding to learning • Recording information • Revising and editing • Using ongoing assessments • Journaling
Small Groups	• Brainstorming • Designing posters • Making a group response sheet • Plotting on a graphic organizer • Writing in various genres • Gathering research	• Problem solving • Charting learning responses • Taking notes • Revising and editing • Working on projects • Assessing

T: Total Group

Use total group presentations when the entire class needs to hear the information in a consistent manner. For example, students may need to receive the same guidelines, rules, or directions. Lecturettes are effective formats for dispensing information to the total class. Interweaving discussions and guided practice with the information is more effective than presenting information alone. Use total groups when individuals or small groups report on a specific topic segment, share a report, present a project, and celebrate learning.

A: Alone

Students who are strong in intrapersonal intelligence learn best when working alone. Students need to work alone to process information, to show what they know, to develop responsibility, and to assume ownership of learning. However, they need to work with others to develop social skills. All authors need to work alone on some assignments. Most writing is completed independently in the real world, so each student needs to become a competent writer.

P: Partner

Some teachers ask, "Why do I need to ask students to work with a partner?" It has been the norm to place students in groups of threes or fours for group work. Many assignments work better with two students, however. Partner work provides more opportunity for each student to be actively engaged and participate. Think about it! During a writing assignment, if partners pass a paper back and forth between them, each one is writing, thinking, discussing, sharing answers, and responding and engaging during the assignment. Students who prefer to work alone need to learn to work cooperatively. It is easier for these students to work with a partner than to work in a larger group.

Partner Writing Ideas

Duo Writing

Assign partners A and B.

1. Provide a topic.

2. Partner A writes.

3. A signal is given.

4. Partner B reads and makes suggestions.

5. Continue repeating steps 2, 3, and 4.

6. Partners read their stories and revise them to create a flow of ideas.

Drawing Duet

1. Partner A draws one item or scene from the current study.

2. Partner B adds to the picture.

3. Partners exchange roles until the drawing is complete.

4. Partners discuss the drawing and write the important facts as a border.

5. The partners sign the drawing and display it.

Build a Crossword

1. Partner A writes a key word from the topic vocabulary in the center of the paper.

2. Partner B builds another word to attach it to one of the letters.

3. Partners A and B take turns until the puzzle is formed using the unit's key words.

4. Partners make up the clues and write them on an index card or separate sheet of paper.

Give a response form similar to the one shown in Figure 4.14 to partners to process content information after a reading assignment. The students identify the most important information in the beginning, middle and end of the passage. They also decide who will be the illustrator and who will be the author.

Figure 4.14   Responding After Reading

Beginning	Middle	End
Illustrate it.	Illustrate it.	Illustrate it.
Write about it.	Write about it.	Write about it.

S: Small Group

A student learns from conversation with other individuals. By discussing, sharing, and creating together, an effective small group pulls on the individual talents of the team members to complete the assignment successfully. Often the student who enjoys learning with other people is referred to as a "social butterfly." This learner is strong in interpersonal intelligence and processes information by sharing and finding listening ears.

Point Highlights

Students in small groups identify one or two important facts or points for each member to highlight on a mini poster. Encourage students to use graffiti-style writing, bright colors, and unique designs to place the points in long-term memory.

Fact Rap

1. Each group member reads the passage and writes three important facts to remember.

2. Individuals take turns reading and sharing their facts.

3. The group discusses and identifies one important fact for each team member.

4. Each student creates a two-line rap for his or her fact.

5. All lines of the rap are written on a large sheet of paper and displayed.

6. The group presents the fact rap. The class joins the group and repeats the fact rap.

Sequence Showcase

Assign a reading passage in the current study that contains a procedure or sequence. Give each student in the group a transparency and markers.

1. Students discuss the passage and identify the steps in the procedure or the sequence of events.

2. Each student becomes responsible for one segment of the procedure or sequence. The details are written on a transparency.

3. Students use the overhead to present the process or sequence in order to the class or to another group.

SUMMARY

Use novel strategies and activities to teach the terminology related to the writing craft. When students have opportunities to apply the skills and use the terms in processing conversations or discussions, they become more confident, productive writers.

The steps in the writing process give the student a guide to follow in writing brief passages and essays. Each learner needs prior knowledge and experiences related to the writing topic to be successful. Require more first drafts than final copies because this stage guides the student to record the creative ideas and facts stored in memory. The revision stage gives the writer an opportunity to enhance the passage. In the editing step, the student applies learned mechanical skills. The final copy is a reflection of the author's best work at this time in his or her writing journey. Flexible grouping strategies add variety to writing lessons while meeting individual needs. Design each grouping scenario to provide experiences for each young author to be successful in academic and personal writing activities.

INSTRUCTIONAL STRATEGIES AND ACTIVITIES FOR THE DIFFERENTIATED WRITING CLASSROOM 5

The migratory patterns of butterflies are innate.

Learning strategies become internalized guides for authors.

TEACH EACH WRITING STRATEGY STRATEGICALLY

Educators know that a learning strategy is a procedure used for learning and applying new information. Students need time to encode important information, to connect it to prior knowledge, and to practice using it in problem solving (Siegler, 2004). A young author must learn how to use each writing strategy thoroughly to apply it as needed.

Students need to know how and when to use different writing strategies. Teach each approach strategically and explicitly. Explain and demonstrate each step with the thinking that accompanies each one. When students hear the teacher's thinking, they learn how to organize their own thoughts as they work with a writing strategy. Guide and monitor practice sessions until students apply the strategy automatically. When they master the skill, their oral thinking becomes the guiding self-talk for writing experiences.

This chapter provides a wealth of writing strategies and activities. We begin by looking at the value of using writing to develop critical thinking before, during, and after a lesson. The needs of English-language learners (ELL) are addressed, and we consider the many different formats and genres used in developing engaging writing assignments. We then present a variety of writing strategies, such as brainstorming, journaling, and processing information, to enhance learning. The chapter ends with suggestions for assignment activities from A to Z.

INFORMATIONAL TEXT WRITING AND CRITICAL THINKING

Interpreting and thinking critically about factual information are valuable components of learning in every classroom. The National Commission on Writing (2003) emphasized this point: "Developing critical thinkers and writers should be understood as one of the central works of education" (p. 32). Writing assignments are designed to perfect thinking skills before, during, and after instruction.

An effective lesson is based on the learners' prior knowledge and experience. For example, before a topic, skill, or concept is introduced, learners are asked to share what they know about the information. Often the preassessment activity involves writing. Later, during a lesson, writing activities are assigned for the student to apply, process, and gain understanding of the new information. Finally, at the end of instructional segments, teachers give writing assessments and evaluations to find out which facts, concepts, or skills are interpreted or understood. The post-assessment also reveals how students are taking ownership of the new learning.

Across content areas, learners receive assignments daily requiring written interpretations, explanations, opinions, or responses to questions about the topic. Here are some examples of informational writing activities:

- Define the following terms and concepts.
- Recall supporting details for the main idea.
- Solve the problem. Explain the steps used to find the solution.
- Interpret the directions and instructions.
- Explain the information in your own words.
- Clarify the meaning of _____.
- Ask or answer questions.
- List the steps and describe the procedure.
- Interpret facts and data.
- Distinguish facts from opinions.
- Examine causes and effects.
- Make a prediction.
- Draw conclusions.
- Summarize.
- Relate the new facts to your life.
- Gather and interpret data.

Figure 5.1 lists more writing activities students will encounter in the verbal/auditory, visual, and tactile areas. Identify the activities you have used with a checkmark. Place an X beside the activities you want to add to your instruction toolbox.

Figure 5.1	Assignment Activities for Writing Informational Text	
Verbal/Auditory	*Visual*	*Tactile*
☐ Sequence the important events. ☐ Write the beginning/middle/end. ☐ Outline the passage. ☐ Write a new ending. ☐ Assign a new title and subtitles to the chapter. ☐ Give facts, opinions, or inferences based on the text. ☐ Create a postcard about a character. ☐ Tell how characters felt when. . . . ☐ Summarize text. ☐ Compare and contrast. ☐ Critique. ☐ Debate an issue. ☐ Write a position statement. ☐ Pretend you are interviewing the inventor. Write the questions and answers. ☐ Explain the problem or conflict in the story. ☐ Answer the questions about the text. ☐ Write a fact song or poem. ☐ Select background music to match the main idea. ☐ Design a book report. ☐ Write a rap about the setting. ☐ Analyze an event. ☐ Write an autobiography for a character. ☐ Write a letter to a character. ☐ Relate facts to today or self. ☐ List important facts. ☐ Add details to notes. ☐ Journal.	☐ Design a book cover. ☐ Create a collage. ☐ Study and interpret charts, pictures, graphs, and other visuals. ☐ Draw a pictorial representation. ☐ Create a caricature. ☐ Make a flipbook. ☐ Create a design to display a word. ☐ Make a poster or banner. ☐ Design a flow map of the sequence. ☐ Develop a time line. ☐ Make a crossword puzzle with vocabulary words. ☐ Illustrate. ☐ Design an advertisement. ☐ Draw an editorial cartoon. ☐ Plot facts on a graphic organizer. ☐ Draw the setting. ☐ Create a cartoon strip. ☐ Make an acrostic poem. ☐ Create a character map. ☐ Develop a storyboard. ☐ Draw a character and write his or her attributes. ☐ Create an advertisement.	☐ Create a reenactment. ☐ Direct a simulation. ☐ Walk a sequence. ☐ Demonstrate a concept. ☐ Role-play events or people. ☐ Complete an experiment. ☐ Go on a scavenger hunt. ☐ Design a model. ☐ Play a game. ☐ Go on a field trip. ☐ Complete a center activity. ☐ Draw a cartoon about the conflict and resolution. ☐ Play a skill game. ☐ Create a motion to remember a fact or vocabulary word. ☐ Use letter tiles to create vocabulary. ☐ Design a diorama. ☐ Create a collage using important facts. ☐ Create a display for a bulletin board. ☐ Create a dance to teach the facts. ☐ Design a game board using key words. ☐ Play competitive games with facts.

WRITING STRATEGIES FOR ENGLISH-LANGUAGE LEARNERS

Culturally responsive teachers become familiar with English-language learners' background and needs. These students often respond to visuals, demonstrations or modeling, and music.

Reyes and Vallone (2008) recommended three ways to teach English-language learners a new skill: (1) use a context-embedded demonstration, (2) give appropriate linguistic support, and (3) provide a stress-free environment. Immediately following the demonstration, engage the learner using manipulatives or hands-on experiences. Verbalize each step or procedure during the modeling process and practice sessions. Guide the students to see mistakes and errors as learning opportunities.

Use the following suggestion to assist an English-language learner with writing strategies:

- Use pictures with the words and phrases written in the student's native language and in English.
- Provide a peer or adult to interpret and record the student's ideas.
- Provide books and supplementary materials available in the learner's first language and at the appropriate reading level.
- Use the language experience approach.
- Become familiar with the student's background so you can plan personalized writing activities.
- Ask the student to create displays reflecting his or her customs or holidays. Add writing assignments that include labeling and explanations.
- Encourage the student to write questions and concerns for an interpreter.
- Accept writing containing a combination of English and the student's first language.
- Demonstrate appreciation; honor the student in all writing activities.
- If possible, provide a peer who speaks the student's first language as a learning partner during writing activities.

Nessel and Dixon (2008) offered the following guidelines for writing instruction for ELLs, noting that these guidelines are relevant for all students:

- Have students write about personally meaningful topics.
- Make sure that thinking and talking precede writing.
- Emphasize writing as a communication tool.
- Relate writing assignments to other texts and language activities.
- Have students share their writing.
- Engage students in a wide variety of writing activities.
- Respond to errors with sensitivity.

DIFFERENTIATING WRITING WITH FORMATS AND GENRES

Unique formats and genres intrigue and motivate students. By using a variety of these, students learn different ways to communicate through writing. The teacher who challenges students to use various writing forms and genres to learn, report, and process information takes the "same old way," or the ruts, out of teaching in the content areas.

Provide students with exciting, novel ways to think about content information. When facts, concepts, and ideas are applied in a distinctive writing format, they will be remembered. Each genre or format presents a different way to record and retain information. Formats and genres are listed in Figure 5.2. Formats and genres are listed in the following section with brief explanations to share with students when each style of writing is introduced. Challenge students to add more ideas to the list.

Figure 5.2 Formats and Genres				
Literary Genres				
Narrative:				
Story	Autobiography	Novel	Biography	Diary
Fable	Ghost story	Historical fiction	Comedy	Fantasy
Myths	Nursery rhymes	Cartoons	Jokes	
Sports stories	War stories	Westerns	Mystery/Suspense	
Nonnarrative:				
Arguments	Essays	Debates	Position statements	Speeches
Play	Poems	Skits	Songs	References
Nonliterary Genres				
Transactional:				
Letters	Interview	Invitations	Leaflets	Postcard
Procedural:				
Directions	Procedures	Lists	Rules	Recipes	Instructions
Reports:				
For the media	Investigations	Reviews	Keys	
Meeting minutes	Graphic organizers	Time lines/ tables		
Expository:				
Lecturettes	Surveys	Questionnaires	Inventories	Explanations
Press releases				
Persuasive:				
Essays	Editorials	Proposals	Advertisements	
Complaints	Platform statements			

Format Showcase

The following formats engage students in writing experiences to process content information. Each writing strategy can challenge young authors and showcase their skills. Select an approach and tailor it to the individual's needs. Use the strategies used in learning centers, as daily tasks, or as homework assignments.

Advertisements, Jingles, Songs, and Poems

The advertising world uses commercials that place words to a beat in jingles, songs, and poems to make us remember products. Use these tools to enhance learners' memory of details and facts. Ask students to replace the familiar words with important content information. As they rehearse and perform their rhythmic creation, the topic information moves into long-term memory.

Autobiography

An autobiography is a story or book an individual writes about his or her own life. Use a survey or questionnaire to gather information for the activity. Students usually enjoy this personalized writing experience. When the skill is mastered, ask students to take on the role of a character in a content study and create an autobiography for the individual.

Biography

A biography is a story or book written about someone's life. The information for the passage, story, or book usually comes from extended research or interviews.

Book Review

A book review presents the student's opinion about a book he or she has read. The key points, the highlights, and the best and worst features of the book are discussed.

Calendars and Day Planners

Calendars and day planners record daily schedules, appointments, to-do lists, phone numbers, and personal goals. Students may keep calendars or logs to post school events, important things to remember, and assignments.

Cartoons and Comic Strips

Use the humor of cartoons and comic strips to make mundane information and concepts come alive. Humor enhances learning, relieves stress, and reduces tension for individuals of all ages. Ask students to create comic strips or cartoons using the information in their unit of study. Artistic talents are tapped as the characters and scenes develop. Have students place the characters' conversations in speech bubbles to elicit interpretation of emotions and feelings. The scenes will reflect the learners' understanding of the information.

Cartoons and comic strips are effective tools to use to compare and contrast new facts, to show humor in situations, and to illustrate facts and opinions. Use editorial cartoons to teach skills for promoting a point of view. The creation of each frame reveals how the student interprets and understands the information. Writing assignments that use cartoons and comic strips are popular because students enjoy connecting humor and learning.

Dialogue

Ask the student to write and role-play the conversations of characters. The dialogue will reflect the writer's interpretations of facts, personalities, and emotions. Record the character's words in various situations and time periods. Assign the role of inventor, botanist, astronaut, hero, archeologist, historian, family member, friend, mathematician, artist, actor, or other individual in the unit of focus.

Remember objects or living things may be personified using dialogue. For example, record an opal conversing with an emerald or a tree in the rain forest chatting with a tree in the desert.

E-mail, Blogs, and Text Messaging

E-mails, blogs, and text messages are popular communicating tools used by students in their daily lives. Use these techniques for tutoring, homework, notes, interviews, or research. This technology is in almost every home and business. The messages are in a shorthand language with which students feel comfortable. These modern communicating media give students experiences they enjoy while preparing them for tomorrow's world.

Lists

Use lists to alphabetize, categorize, chunk, sequence, and sort information. Jotting items down usually makes them easier to remember. Information in a list is easier to recall than words or phrases in sentence form. For example, grocery needs are placed on lists, and many individuals make to-do lists and check off each item as it is completed. Some people make mental lists to accomplish tasks.

Magazine and Newspaper Articles

Writing an article for a favorite magazine or newspaper gives the student a chance to write on a topic of interest. If possible, encourage the author to choose the place for publication. Obtain parent approval before submitting anything for publication. The student does not have to submit an article to meet a writing goal and enjoy the experience.

Photo Essays

Remember the saying: A picture is worth a thousand words. Write a detailed report about an individual or a group of people, an event, concept, or discovery in picture form. The pictures may have captions or dialogue to provide more information. The pictures may be photographs, cutouts, drawings, or a combination. Photos may be used to illustrate a procedure or directions. It is fun to assign photo essays as follow-up activities for a special study or a field trip.

Predictions

Predictions are guesses about what will happen next. Write predictions for experiments, text passages, or events. The guesses foster thinking, and students become intrigued, wondering if their predictions are correct. Honor all guesses and engage the learners in discussions about reasons the predictions or ideas will or will not work. Prediction skills are used in the thinking classroom.

Profiles

Profiles are detailed reports or outlines of an event or incident. They describe an individual or a group of people. Profiles may include the highlights of a person's life or give a detailed description of an event.

Sitcoms

Students are interested in television sitcoms, so use these programs to spark writing ideas. For instance, they can take notes and identify the main idea and supporting details of a favorite episode. Use sitcoms to apply writing skills and strategies. Remember, students need parent approval to watch the sitcoms.

USING PERSONIFICATION TO PROCESS CONTENT INFORMATION

Personification gives physical abilities, behaviors, and other characteristics of human beings to plants, animals, and nonliving things. Provide several examples of personification. The student will eagerly apply personification to process content information.

Example 1: The Trail of Tears

- Subject: History
- Topic: The Trail of Tears
- Genre: Historical Fiction

The road remembered the shuffle of moccasins and the teardrops that fell. She knew the Cherokee Indians were being herded on a long, forced walking journey from their homes in the East to their new reservations in the West. The road could hear the sadness in the Indian voices. She could hear the cries of babies as they bounced along on the backs of their weary mothers. The road knew why she would always be remembered as the Trail of Tears.

Example 2: Cule E. Mol Goes Underground

- Subject: Science
- Topic: Diffusion
- Genre: Mystery
- Vocabulary bonus: The name *Cule E. Mol* was created from scrambling the syllables in *molecule*, a vocabulary word.

His name is Cule E. Mol. He is a water molecule. He is on the FBI's "Most Wanted" list. Cule E. Mol was last seen condensing with his friends as they came to earth disguised as raindrops.

It is believed that he went underground and entered the root of a tree with a group of his molecule cohorts. They were traced moving through the root. They diffused to travel separately through the stems and leaves. The large plant will be indicted for using osmosis to harbor the fugitives.

The FBI plans to take Cule E. Mol into custody before he evaporates and escapes. If he is not captured, Cule E. Mol is expected to travel on wind currents to another continent and condense there. He may be camouflaged on an ice cap, flow with the current of a great river, or continue his condensing and evaporating escapades.

PLANNING FOR INDIVIDUAL NEEDS

Teachers in the differentiated classroom plan their students' writing experiences with careful attention to individual needs. Choice boards, agendas, individualized writing assignments, and the language experience approach can be customized and used strategically to intervene and address identified needs.

Choice Boards

Use choice boards for students to select various ways to work with their information. Adapt the following examples of choice boards to use as needed. The "wild card" is an optional space for a student who prefers to think of another way to work with the information. The teacher approves the student's wild card idea. The approval request can be placed in a choice submission basket on the teacher's desk.

Example

1. Name _____ Date _____ Topic _____

2. Student: My Wild Card activity pick is _____ .

3. Teacher approval (check one)

   ____Yes

   ____Yes, with the following change _____.

   ____ No

4. Teacher Signature or Initials: _____ Date: _____

Writing Thinking Boxes

This choice board, shown in Figure 5.3, is designed to apply different levels of thinking to differentiate assignments. These offerings challenge students to use high-level thinking skills to develop as problem solvers and thinkers.

Figure 5.3 Writing Thinking Boxes	
Level I: Knowledge	**Level II: Comprehension**
• Write the step-by-step sequence of a procedure or event. • Tell about it in your own words.	• Interpret and illustrate the passage in your own words. • List some examples of each fact.
Level III: Application	**Level IV: Analysis**
• Demonstrate a way to use _____. • Use the data to solve the problem.	• If _____, then _____. • Make a graph to display the parts.
Level V: Synthesis	**Level VI: Evaluation**
• Use the new facts to create an original plan. • Develop a new way to _____.	• Design an ad for the best use of a product. • Evaluate the new information and decide how it will benefit others.

Bingo Choice

The bingo choice board example, shown in Figure 5.4, gives students options for a variety of ways to write. The student selects activities, or the teacher assigns activities to individuals or small groups.

Figure 5.4   Bingo Choice Board

	A	B	C	D	E
1	Create a cartoon showing a conversation between a movie hero and a fairy tale character.	Recommend a television show to everyone. Write a review of it. Tell why you selected the show.	Write an advertising jingle for your favorite food.	Think of a new invention to help you study. Draw it. Write a description for a magazine article.	Write the directions for your favorite sport or hobby. Illustrate them.
2	List five of your favorite books. Rewrite the ending of one of the books.	Pretend you are interviewing your hero on a talk show. Write a script for the show.	Create a flip book to describe many uses for an empty can. Illustrate each page.	Use a Venn diagram to compare and contrast two of your favorite pastimes.	Create a poster to "sell" your friends on reading your favorite book.
3	Pretend you are a millionaire for a day. Write a diary entry about your lucky day.	Design a postcard describing your town. Write a note on the card telling someone why he or she should visit you.	WILD CARD	If you were twice as tall, what would you do? Write a poem about the adventure.	Find your favorite topic in the encyclopedia. Make an outline of the topic.
4	Survey classmates about their favorite ice cream flavors. Create a chart with the results. Write a summary for the class newsletter.	Write a newspaper article describing your greatest fear.	Name a wild animal found in your state. Create a concept map related to the animal.	If you could change one part of your day, what would it be? Explain your reasons.	Read about your favorite pet. Create a shape book to present facts about the pet.
5	Develop your platform to persuade your parents to buy the new game you want.	Invent a new way to carry out your least favorite chore.	Write a training manual to teach someone how to play your favorite sport or game.	Create a PowerPoint presentation about your school, home, town, or state.	Write a song to a familiar tune, rap, or poem to describe facts about a person, place, or thing in the current study.

Choice Tic-Tac-Toe

Figure 5.5 is a choice board for an agenda assignment or a writing center. The student may select one activity on the board to complete in one session or a row to complete over a period of time.

Figure 5.5 Choice Tic-Tac-Toe		
	A	*B*	*C*
I	Design a bookmark with a list of your favorite book characters.	List three things you like about a room in your house. Write a note to your parent or guardian telling how you would like to change the room.	Name your favorite vehicle. Use 10 words to describe how it moves.
2	Write a note telling someone why he or she is special.	WILD CARD	Write a poem about your favorite television program.
3	Read about your favorite animal. Draw it. Write five sentences that tell why it would or would not be a good pet.	Name an insect you see often. Find five new facts and make a statement about each one. Draw it. Label the insect's parts.	Choose three objects in your classroom. Write three short sentences as "What Am I?" clues for the objects. Ask a friend to name each object from the clues.

"It" Board

The choice board shown in Figure 5.6 is used with a specific topic, concept, or vocabulary word. Identify an important fact, item, important person, place, event, or invention to use as "It." These generic activities can be used across the content areas.

Figure 5.6 "It" Board		
	A	*B*	*C*
I	Draw and label it.	Write a poem about it.	Compare it with something else.
2	Write to someone and persuade him or her that it is needed.	WILD CARD	Name it and write an ad to sell it.
3	Write a story or play, making it the main character.	Pretend it just became a new member of our class. Write a set of rules that it must follow.	Create a best friend for it. Write a conversation between the two at their first meeting.

Agendas

An agenda is given to students who need specific assignments. The agenda is a list of selected or designed activities for the learner or small group of learners who do not need to work on the lesson for the total group. Each item on the list teaches the standards on the student's ability level using a stimulating, challenging activity in the learner's area of interest. Busywork is not included. A time line is set for completion of the work. As each task is completed, it may be placed in an agenda folder. The student keeps a checklist or reflection log in the folder, too. The reflections may be used as assessment pieces. An agenda can become part of a customized contract for the learner's needs.

There are many advantages of using an agenda with a student. The writing assignments are designed to match the student's individual needs. The student is able to work at his or her own pace and can choose the task order but has a set period of time to complete the tasks. The independent work fosters self-directed learning.

An agenda may be designed for a small group when the learners have similar needs. The students may work cooperatively or independently as needed on the tasks.

Agenda Ideas

- Complete a computer program.
- Listen to taped information. Write a summary, critique, or editorial for it.
- Plot information on a graphic organizer. Then write or draw the sequence of events or procedures for an experiment using the organizer.
- Complete a list of three to five writing activities within a specified time.
- Select a row or column of writing activities from a choice board.

Individualized Writing Projects

A student may have an independent writing project as an alternative assignment. A project has a set goal and purpose. It poses an essential question to answer, hypothesis to prove, or problem to solve. The project gives the learner an opportunity to gain in-depth knowledge of a topic. The topic or subtopic is selected by the student with a contract, or it is assigned by the teacher. An established time line and rubric are set at the beginning of the project so expectations are identified. To accompany the written requirement, the student needs the opportunity to demonstrate the learning and understanding gained from the project with a performance assessment such as a graphic, a musical composition, a role-play, or an interview. More information about contracts, brainstorming, researching, and note taking is included later in this chapter.

Language Experience Activities

In a language experience activity, the teacher writes a student's exact statements word for word. The teacher records the statements of one or more students as they contribute their thoughts to form a list, a discussion, or a story. Each student observes as the teacher records his or her words.

Language experiences demonstrate the writing and reading connection. The learner observes the letters forming words, the words making sentences, and sentences creating paragraphs. Seeing the words created as they are scripted is the most valuable component of the language experience approach. Write the words on chart paper, an overhead, a dry-erase board, or a computer screen. We recommend chart paper because it is easy to handle, move, display, and revisit as needed.

Students gather near the teacher so they see the words as they are written. The teacher repeats each student's words as they are written. This models how the spoken words are transferred to written words. Students may not understand that what they say can become words written on the paper. Explain that this is writing! Learners may know the words they want to say but not be able to write them. Language-experience activities train students to write words as they say them. This writing strategy is effective with individuals, small groups, or a total class. The teacher may need to guide the learner in reading the written passage.

Clear communication lines are vital to productive work with language-experience activities. Create a risk-free environment so each student feels free to express himself or herself. Let the student know it is important for everyone to hear, know, and understand all statements.

Use probing statements and questions to elicit explanations that clarify statements. Here are some examples:

- Tell me more.

- What part do you not understand?

- Explain this _____.

- What does _____ mean?

Language Experience for the Emergent Learner

The teacher usually selects the topic for the language experience. The class can choose a title before the writing begins, or a catchy, clever title can be chosen at the end of the story.

Students give the information orally to the teacher. The teacher writes the sentence, saying the name of each letter as it is formed. The students repeat the name of the letter. For example, if a student's sentence began with the letter *T,* the teacher says "Capital *T.*" The student repeats it: "Capital *T.*" When the letters have formed a word, the teacher and the student say the word together. For example, "Capital *T-h-e* spells *The.*" Using this method, the teacher reinforces the recognition of each letter's name and every word and all connecting words to make a sentence. When a sentence is complete, the teacher reads the sentence while the students listen. The students repeat the sentence as the teacher moves a pointer under each word as it is read.

As learners become more proficient with letter recognition, spelling, and reading, their progress is evident. Students' voices join the teacher's voice as they say the letters and words as they appear.

When a chart is complete, the students and the teacher read the entire story, passage, or list together. The teacher may need to read one sentence at a time and ask the students to repeat it. The experience ends with the oral reading. As students read and hear the words on the chart, they gain an understanding of the writing and reading connection.

The same process is used when a student in the early stages of writing composes a journal passage. The student needs someone to write each line as it is being said.

Language Experience in the Upper Grades

Language experience activities are effective in the upper grades. When the teacher records the words of a student, it becomes a language experience. Use this procedure on the board, an overhead, or a computer projection screen to record student responses during a small-group or class discussion.

The teacher models the thinking skills needed to answer questions related to the reading or the discussion. The teacher demonstrates thinking step-by-step. For example, a student realizes that as he or she speaks, the teacher is scripting the words. As the words are said orally, the student learns to write them. Teachers say students often know answers but cannot transfer the information to test forms. Language experience activities develop metacognitive writing skills needed for academic and test success.

The chart in Figure 5.7 lists skills and suggests assignments for students at different levels of mastery in understanding the reading and writing connection. A language experience activity is recommended to develop this awareness.

Figure 5.7   Language Experience Chart: Adjustable Assignments

B	• Increases personal sight-reading vocabulary. • Transfers this skill to note taking.	• Develops an understanding of word-to-sentence construction. • Adds to the mastered word list.	• Has more opportunities to see words in print. • Follows words in print as the information is read aloud. • Sees words written and spelled as they are spoken. • Develops a letter-to-word connection.
A	• Writes and reads the story as a leading contributor to the language experience process. • Has a strong knowledge base of language and sentence construction. • Usually spells the word before the teacher writes the word. • Is a fluent, comprehending reader.	• Sees spoken words in print. • Contributes to the story or topic. • Recognizes and knows how to spell most common words. • Reads many words without assistance.	• Can repeat sentences after someone reads them aloud. • Knows a few words for writing. • Prefers to use words for speaking. • Has minimal confidence in writing ability.
	High Degree of Mastery	*Approaching Mastery*	*Beginning Mastery*

Key:

A. What does each group know now?

B. What does this group need to know next?

WRITING STRATEGIES

Effective teachers incorporate a variety of strategies and carefully plan assignments to ensure that their students use writing as a tool for learning. Whether students are involved in simple journaling tasks or extended research projects, writing solidifies, deepens, and extends students' content learning. Mix and match the following methods to develop meaningful assignments.

Brainstorming

For me the initial delight is in the surprise of remembering something I didn't know I knew.

—Robert Frost

Brainstorming involves recording each thought that comes to mind when a word or topic is presented. This thinking strategy teaches the student how to bring thoughts and ideas out of memory storage. As ideas are expressed, each is listed so it can be considered for use in the writing assignment. Brainstorming triggers the mind to recall related words, facts, visual images, sounds, and feelings. For example, when a ride at the fair is recalled as a pleasant experience, excitement is evident. If the experience was unpleasant, negative emotions are apparent. Involve the class, a group, or individuals in brainstorming activities.

Use the following suggested guidelines for a brainstorming session:

- Give students a quiet time to list their thoughts independently. This is a handy tip because the list makes it easier for the individual to contribute to a brainstorming session.
- Form brainstorming partners or teams.
- Challenge the teams to share, honor, and list each suggested item to produce a quantity of ideas.
- Tell the teams to move the list from an emphasis on quantity to an emphasis on quality by prioritizing the list. Model this step, showing students how to number the items in order of importance.
- Demonstrate ways to justify the importance and order of each item on the list. Use the following prompts to assist the teams with the prioritizing step:

  The best _____.

  The most important items are _____.

  The ideas that make the most sense are _____.

  The most interesting items or ideas are _____

  The similar items to combine are _____.

  The unimportant items are _____.

(See "Idea Roundup: Crucial Collections" in the "Step 1. Getting Started: Prewriting" section of Chapter 4.)

Mental Shopping

My brain has more space than any store.

Its shelves make room for thoughts galore!

I can shop for facts and ideas in my mind.

Information I have stored is easy to find.

—Chapman and King

Brainstorming Guidelines

Use the following guidelines to make a brainstorming activity successful.

- Work in small groups.
- Tell individuals to jot down two or three ideas
- Assign a recorder to list the ideas.
- Encourage "piggybacking" on ideas.
- Tell teams to accept all responses.
- Ask teams to select the top ten or best responses.
- Give groups time to categorize listed items to link details and create order.
- Tell the teams to cluster their thoughts by plotting them on a graphic organizer.
- Create a class list as items are discussed.

Prompts to Jump-Start Thinking

Prompts are statements or questions that focus the students' attention on a topic and stimulate, or "jump-start," their thinking. One of the most common problems teachers face during writing assignments is assisting students who say, "I don't know what to say," or, "I don't know how to start." Use prompts to generate ideas for writing experiences.

Prompt suggestions are provided in the following sections to use in general surveys and subject area activities. Select the jump-start prompts to enhance the lesson and adapt them for individual needs.

If students work in pairs or groups to respond to the prompts, they can produce one paper. If one response sheet is required, each group member may need a copy of the work for an individual journal or portfolio.

Survey Prompts

I like _____ because _____.

My favorite thing to do is _____ because _____.

I become upset when _____.

The best thing my teachers do is _____ because _____.

After school, I _____.

I am happy when _____ because _____.

Ten years from now, I want to _____.

Feeling Prompts

Writing is difficult for me when _____.

I do not like writing activities when _____.

During writing activities, I feel _____.

I like to write about _____ because _____.

Book Report Prompts

When I read, I _____.

My favorite book is _____ because _____.

My least favorite topic to read about is _____ because _____.

When I read, I need _____.

The best book character I know is _____ because _____.

Content Prompts

Today I learned _____.

The steps I need to remember are _____.

My favorite part of the lesson was _____.

I need to remember _____.

This _____ reminds me of _____ because _____.

The best way for me to remember the _____ is _____.

The most important facts to remember are _____.

My favorite person in this passage is _____.

If _____ were happening today, I think _____.

What do you think about _____? Why?

What do you think will happen next?

When _____ happened, how did the people feel? Why?

If you were _____, what would you do? Why? How?

Jump-Start Prompts

I found the answer by _____.

Compare _____ and _____.

The steps I used to solve this problem are _____.

The easiest part of the problem was _____.

What does _____ mean to you?

As I read the passage, I learned _____.

Here is what I know about the topic:_____.

I would choose _____ as the answer because _____.

My opinion on the issue is_____.

Words just float here and there in my mind,

When I search for them, they're easy to find.

—Chapman and King

Journaling

Journaling is a way for a student to write freely to place thoughts, feelings, and ideas on paper. It often becomes a form of therapy, giving an individual the opportunity to express privately what is on his or her mind. Journaling can be an exciting addition to most units of study. Remember, the more an individual writes, the more skills are perfected. Journaling incorporates meaningful writing practice into daily activities. Use the following suggestions as journal formats for processing and recording information in the content areas.

Photo Scrapbook Journals

Use photos, pictures from magazines, or pictures drawn by the students to illustrate thoughts, ideas, reflections, and facts learned. Add caption to explain the visuals and create links to the information studied. Information comes alive in picture form. Captions give the learner writing practice with subject terminology.

Comic Journals

Comic journals contain cartoons, jokes, or riddles to illustrate the events, characters, and facts in the unit. Humor combined with art is an exciting way to interpret and retain information. Use captions to add humor to the content. Use this activity to express opinions, as in editorial cartoons.

Content Journals

Content journals record information learned about topics through reading, hands-on experiences, videos, demonstrations, projects, field trips, research, and other sources. Use entries to process, review, or share information.

"What Are You Thinking?" Journals

"What Are You Thinking?" journals give the student opportunities to reflect on step-by-step thinking processes. Include illustrations and explanations. In math classrooms, use this metacognitive journal to record the steps for solving a problem. During a science lesson, write the procedures for an experiment in this special journal. Challenge the author to explain the self-talk or thinking while completing a hands-on project.

EQ (Emotional Quotient) Journals

In an EQ journal, the student records feelings and emotions during a unit of study, an experience, or an assignment. The date, time, place, and experience are noted as part of each entry. Use prompts for EQ journal entries, such as the following:

- Today's lesson reminds me of the color _____ because _____.
- As I worked, I enjoyed _____. I did not like_____.
- When I am working on _____, I feel like _____ because _____.
- The theme song for this lesson is _____ because _____.
- My "Aha!" is _____.

Log Journals

Log journals record the events of a project, a study, an adventure, or a discovery. They usually include the date when information is explored, discovered, or learned. Personal insights, reflections, hypotheses, and thoughts are a crucial part of the log experience.

Partner Journals

Partner journals use paper divided into two equal parts. One student writes a journal entry on one side of the paper. The partner responds on the opposite side, making comments on the topics addressed. In most cases, the student chooses or is assigned a trusted partner so ideas, questions, and thoughts are shared freely.

Example

Date/Student's Entry	Date/Partner's Response

Note Journals

Note journals use paper divided into two equal parts. The student writes notes from the study of a section of information on the left-hand side of the page while it is read or discussed. When reviewing the same material, additions and corrections are made to the notes on the right-hand side.

More Journaling Formats and Activities

Here are additional suggestions for varying journal formats to complement special assignments, units, topics, or projects:

"Dear Diary" journal	Survey journal	Data collection journal
Observation journal	Journalist journal	I SPY journal
"Another Voice" journal	Homework log	Technical journal
Scientific journal	Math log	Learning journal
"Roving Reporter Notes"	Response journal	Interview journal
Personal journal	Subject journal	

Write On . . .

Allow students the opportunity to use a variety of writing supplies for journaling. Vary materials with the assignments. Add to the following suggestions. Make journaling an exciting, rewarding learning experience for students so they will say, "Look at my journal!"

Spiral notebook	Loose-leaf notebook	Personalized folder
Clipboard	Day calendar	Shape book
Computer disc	Note pad	Scroll
Legal pad	Diary	Word processor

Create your own "Write On" journals.

Teacher's Role in Journaling

- *Choose the journaling genre, type, shape, and size to fit the assignment and the expectations.* Remember to make the experience novel and interesting with intriguing activities. Vary the writing forms. Think about how the student feels when all assignments and activities have to be completed in the same way in every class. Make assignments appeal to the learner's desire to complete the tasks and learn.

- *Set expectations and guidelines.* If students are to meet specific criteria in their journal activities, make those expectations concise and clear.

- *Foster creativity and expression.* Encourage learners to express their emotions and feelings in their own way. Provide opportunities that promote "thinking outside the box" and higher-order thinking skills. Accept and honor students' ideas.

- *Provide time to think.* Remember, it takes time to think! One learner may enjoy journaling more than others. One student may know more information about the topic and need more time to write. When the interest level is high and curiosity is stirred, the author needs more time to write.

GATHERING RESEARCH

Research involves discovering or finding as much related information as possible about a topic. The important information is organized and recorded. Topics for research are selected from content material. The teacher can present several topics as choice activities for the research assignment. Self-selection of topics and methods attracts and motivates learners.

Teach students how to conduct research strategically and purposefully. Model the research strategy that matches the assignment. There are various research techniques, but students of all ages need to need to know the general skills for gathering information through note taking and journaling. They need to know how to use basic reference materials, such as a glossary, dictionary, and index. Teach students how to conduct Internet searches and cite the sources.

Proposals and Contracts for Research

A *contract* is an agreement between the student and the teacher outlining one or more tasks to complete. The student develops a *proposal* that lists his or her plans for the research assignment, including the topic; the tasks and activities to accomplish; the sources that will be used; the procedures, tools, and methods for completing it; and how the information will be presented. Provide advice and guidance as needed.

The proposal is submitted to the teacher for approval. The teacher accepts the proposal, makes additions or other changes, or rejects it. When the teacher and student reach agreement on the proposal's content, it becomes a contract. Both the teacher and the student sign and date it. Using a contract is an excellent way to differentiate an assignment.

Consider providing a list of topics from which each student will choose a research interest area. Give the student a contract or agreement that specifies how the research will be conducted and reported.

Occasionally, a student may not find a topic of interest on the list. Permit this learner to submit another area of interest for approval on a contract proposal (see Figures 5.8 and 5.9 for sample forms). Keep in mind that the student's proposed topic

---

Figure 5.8   Contract Proposal Form

Dear _____ (Teacher's name),

I would like to write a research report on _____.

I am interested in learning:

a._____   b._____   c._____.

I plan to gather information from _____, _____, and _____.

I plan to write my report in the following form:

_____ Interview _____ Skit _____ Book _____ Poster _____ Charts _____ Multimedia _____ Booklet

Student's Signature _____   Date_____

Figure 5.9   Contract Proposal Form: Online Surfing (Researching the Web)

Name _____   Date _____

Topic _____

Subtopics _____ _____ _____

My search engine will be _____.

I plan to surf the following sites:

_____ _____ _____ _____ _____

Student's Signature _____   Date_____

---

must fit the current study and meet the assignment's criteria. If the majority of the students have an assigned topic, make the same or similar requirements for the class and the individual who is submitting a contract. Having similar expectations minimizes the time needed to assess the work. The student may need advice and guidance. Design the contract so the tasks can be completed with minimal or no assistance.

The teacher or the student writes a *contract agreement*. The contract form outlines the work to accomplish, the time line for completion, general requirements, the sources, and procedures. Figure 5.10 is a suggested contract form.

Figure 5.10   Contract Agreement Form

Name _____   Teacher _____   Date _____

Topic _____   Subject _____

I agree to use the following sources: _____, _____, _____, _____.

The criteria for the assignment are _____, _____, _____, _____.

The format for the report will be _____.

The length of the report is a maximum of _____ pages.

The work is to be completed by _____ (date).

Student signature _____

Teacher signature_____

Teacher's Role in Research: Guidelines

- Present standards and expectations with specific guidelines.
- Teach and model research skills, techniques, and procedures.
- Provide topic choices.
- Provide a checklist.
- Provide an assessment rubric.
- Monitor preset dates throughout the project.
- Provide conference time and feedback.
- Permit the student to choose the presentation form.

Student's Role in Research: Guidelines

- Tell why you are conducting the research.
- Identify your sources, or places where you found the information.
- Gather all the information and data.
- Separate facts from views and opinions.
- Select the most important facts.
- Delete unnecessary facts and ideas.
- Organize the information.
- Write the research results in your own words.
- Decide how to present your findings.

Ways to Research a Topic

Brainstorming	Discussions	Documentaries	Encyclopedia
Interviews	Reading	Surfing the Web	Viewing a movie clip
Journal articles	Newspaper articles	Computer program	

Presenting Research Reports With "Zippidy-Do"

Provide time and materials for the learners to give informative, creative presentations related to their research. Plan experiences for students to prepare reports using the information in different ways.

Most research reports are perceived as boring and stressful. However, conducting and reporting research can be designed as exciting, powerful tools for learning. Develop experts for specific topics. Take advantage of valuable teaching moments when the learner's interest and enthusiasm are high! Differentiate research reports using these suggestions:

• Create diagrams and charts.	• Develop a video presentation.
• Use caricatures.	• Design a galley display.
• Illustrate with a poster.	• Create a computer presentation.
• Develop a game.	• Record a radio skit.
• Create a skit.	• Design a Web page.
• Write a play.	• Create a big book.

Research Conferences

Research conference checkpoints are scheduled periodically during the research process. These meetings are conducted with the teacher, with a partner, or with a small group. A student feels accountable and more responsible when a progress report or sharing session is established. Conference preparations give the learner a sense of ownership for the work. The form in Figure 5.11 can be used to guide the research conference.

Figure 5.11 Research Conference Form

Name _____   Date _____   Teacher _____

Topic _____   Subject _____

My sources were _____, _____, _____, _____.

Here is an overview of my research: _____.

I have completed _____.

I need to work on _____.

My work will be presented in the form of _____.

I will present my research to _____.

Signature/Date _____

Figure 5.12 contains recommended assignments for students at different levels of mastery of research skills.

Figure 5.12 Adjustable Model for Research

B	• Provide choices for research opportunities. • Assign independent time to explore resource materials and gather data. • Work through approved contracts. • Apply information from a wide variety of reference materials.	• Has more opportunities to do research. • Receives feedback at each step of the procedure.	• Provide feedback on progress. • Use a strong prewriting organizer. • Sequence important facts. • Learns how to use references. • Research with the assistance of a peer or an adult.
A	• Uses a variety of materials as resource • Defines and expands topic clearly. • Works independently and productively. • Reflects creativity. • Applies accurate information.	• Uses two or more sources to locate information. • Stays on topic. • Requires little assistance. • Is aware of purpose of research. • Organizes information and materials.	• Uses one source for given topic. • Wanders from the topic. • Requires some ongoing assistance. • Lacks awareness of purpose. • Uses few organization skills.
	High Degree of Mastery	*Approaching Mastery*	*Beginning Mastery*

Standard: To be an effective researcher

Key:

A. What does the student know now?

B. What does the student need to learn next?

NOTE TAKING

Notes assist recall of facts and ideas gathered from reading or listening. As notes are recorded, the brain focuses attention and processes the information. A student may not know how to take notes. This skill must be taught.

The note-taking skills needed for listening and reading are similar. They are presented separately below, because the skills need to be emphasized as students engage in reading or listening activities.

Note-Taking Tips for Listening

Get Ready

- Have a favorite writing implement and paper ready.
- Use your favorite note-taking tools, such as a highlighter and sticky notes.
- Choose a seat that makes the speaker and presentation materials visible.
- Check the area to avoid any interference with hearing.
- Review previous information in your notes, handouts, or the text.

Get Set

- Turn off other thoughts.
- Focus on the speaker's words.
- Anticipate what will be said.

Go

- Be mentally at the "starting line" and ready when the speaker begins.
- Record key points in your own words.
- Use organizers such as lists, outlines, webs, and time lines with your notes.
- Ask yourself questions similar to the following:
  - How will I use this information?
  - What is the best way to record the information to remember it?
- Make notes on repeated or emphasized information.
- Listen for signals that tell you valuable information is coming. These word and phrase cues include the following:
  - "Again, I would like to point out _____."
  - "You need to remember _____."
  - "Make a note of _____."
  - "The steps are _____."
  - "In summary, _____."

- Review the notes. Highlight or use sticky notes on important information, key words, and phrases.

Note-Taking Tips for Reading

As books and materials are read in an information search, it is important to pay attention to the most valuable data and ideas. The following guidelines are useful when taking notes while reading.

Prepare

- Have a favorite writing implement and paper ready.
- Use your most effective tools, such as a highlighter and sticky notes.
- Choose a comfortable place to read.
- Check the area to avoid anything interfering with reading.

Focus

- Turn off other thoughts.
- Concentrate on the reading material.
- Review previous chapters or notes.
- Preview the headings and subtitles.

Write

- Write important information and ideas in your own words.
- Use key words, phrases, or lists.
- Place the information on a graphic organizer, if needed.
- Highlight important facts and details.
- Circle, box, or highlight important words, phrases, or sentences.
- Create special symbols to place beside information to indicate your level of understanding and ability to use the ideas. The symbols give personal feedback and guide self-talk. Examples include the following:

  * I understand this information.

  ∧ I need more explanation here.

  ? I have a question.

  ! I will use this information.

Tips for Creating Research Note Cards

Note cards are used to record information and ideas from a source as the learner gathers research information. Sources are identified on a card because the information must be cited accurately if it is used later in the text or bibliography. Model steps for creating research note cards using the designated style. Figure 5.13 shows a sample note card.

Guidelines for completing research note cards include the following:

- Record information needed for the report.
- Use the back of the card or another card, if needed.
- Begin each new source on a new card.
- Keep cards from the same source together.
- Use your own words to record the information.
- When recording a quote, list the source and the page number.

Teacher's Role in Note Taking

- Model each strategy.
- Share examples.
- Explain purposes and uses of this information-gathering technique.
- Differentiate the various forms of note taking for the different research resources used, which may include encyclopedias, magazines, reference texts, and the Internet.

Figure 5.13   Sample Note Card

Name _____   Teacher_____   Date_____
Topic _____
Title _____ Date of Publication _____
Source _____ Author _____
Publisher _____ Publisher's City and State _____
Volume _____ Page Number _____
Information Gathered: _____
_____
_____
_____

DEVELOPING OUTLINES AND RUBRICS

"On Line" With Outlines

Begin the student's first outline experiences by using lines for the subheadings. The process of filling in the blanks during oral lessons or study sessions provides the learner with successful experiences in the introduction to outlining.

Example

Parts of a Flower

I. Roots   II. Stem
A. _____   A. _____
        1. _____   1. _____
        2. _____   2. _____
        3. _____

B. _____   B. _____
        1. _____   1. _____
        2. _____   2. _____

Rubrics

The student can use the following rubric to indicate the amount of information needed for each subtopic. Use this form to monitor the writer's research progress. Ask the student to place an *X* on the line to indicate the amount of information found on each subtopic.

Subtopic   **Teeny Tiny**   **Gracious Plenty**

   1. _____   ◄──────────────────────►
   2. _____   ◄──────────────────────►
   3. _____   ◄──────────────────────►

So far, I have used the following sources: _____ _____ _____
I plan to use _____.
I am looking for more information on _____.

Research Rubric

The following rubric can be used for a self-evaluation on a research assignment. Ask the student to place an *X* on the line to indicate self-evaluation of each item.

	In the Trenches		**Over the Rainbow**
1. Collected data	◄──────────	──────────►	
2. Used sources effectively	◄──────────	──────────►	
3. Followed the criteria	◄──────────	──────────►	
4. Recorded data accurately	◄──────────	──────────►	
5. Met the project time line	◄──────────	──────────►	

Comments:

WRITING ESSAYS

An essay is a writing selection with a main topic. Each sentence provides details or explanations for the stated topic. Teach students the skills needed for writing an essay. For example, writers need a hook to grab the reader's attention and a topic sentence to state the purpose of the essay. Be cautious when planning essay assignments. Remember, struggling writers need to be successful in forming sentences and creating, organizing, and writing meaningful paragraphs before essays are assigned. Teach, model, and practice each skill.

Prewriting for Organizing Essays

Before students write an essay, they need to know how to gather information for the prewriting experience. They must have sufficient background knowledge or know how to find resources containing the information. Prewriting experiences include creating lists, brainstorming ideas, engaging in a discussion, and conducting research related to the topic.

One of the most effective prewriting strategies is using a graphic to organize and categorize gathered information. After plotting the data, the student uses these categories to begin drafting the paper. An organizer can be used for writing one paragraph or multiple paragraphs. Many essays follow a five-point approach to writing paragraphs (see Figure 5.14).

Handy Dandy Essays

Plan your five paragraphs in the following handy-dandy way!

1. Draw an outline of your hand and place the topic in the palm of it.

2. Place the main idea on the thumb for the first "whoop-di-do" paragraph.

3. Write a supporting detail on each of the three middle fingers. Use these details to design the three middle paragraphs.

4. Write the conclusion on the little finger. Make your little finger touch the thumb to remind you to repeat the main idea or topic in different words in the conclusion. Add a summary and closing remarks. This creates the last paragraph.

Try one of the graphics shown in Figures 5.15, 5.16, 5.17, 5.18, and 5.19 to organize an essay. Note the different shape used for each part. Use a variety of shapes to make the ideas easier to follow. Select a shape that relates to the information. Discuss each shape and its role. Remember, the categories presented here are examples. Adapt them for your current content study.

Figure 5.14   A Five-Point Approach to Writing Paragraphs

Beginning

Name the topic or subject.
Make opening comments.
Use a hook to get the audience's attention.
Introduce the characters, scene, and plot.
Use the surprise element.
Create curiosity. Ask a question.
Bring in the readers' emotions.
Set the stage. Describe the scene.
Introduce the characters.
Write as though you are speaking directly to the reader.
Use a quote.
Use an anecdote or example.
Use unique or interesting information or trivia (facts).
Make an unbelievable or "far-out" statement.

BEGINNING

Middle

Give main points and details.
Use subtopic paragraphs.
Support the subject.
Stay on your topic.
Build the plot or purpose.
Place details in order.
Group details together.

SUBTOPIC A

SUBTOPIC B

SUBTOPIC C

Ending

Make conclusions: Tie up loose ends.
Review or summarize the most important ideas.
Express your overall feelings, thoughts, or conclusions.
Restate the topic in the beginning paragraph.
Tell how the plot was resolved.
Provide a solution.
Make a recommendation.
Repeat the main points in a new way.
Take the reader back to the beginning.

ENDING

Figure 5.15   From Beginning to End

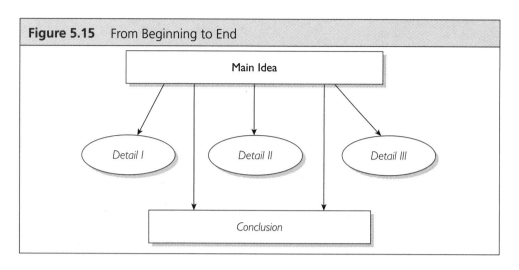

Figure 5.16   The Five *W*s

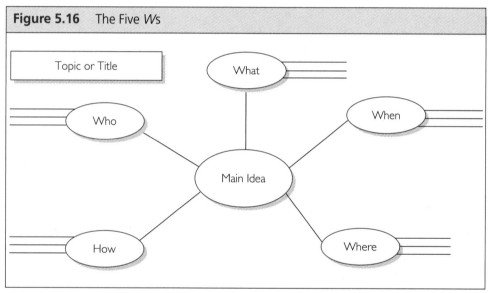

Figure 5.17   Shape Talk

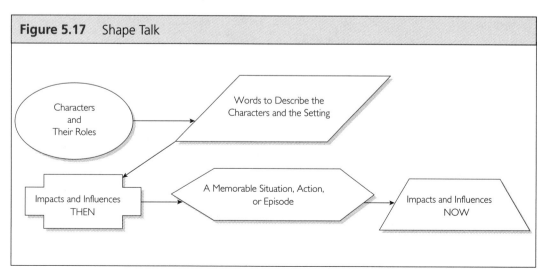

Figure 5.18   Persuasive Writing

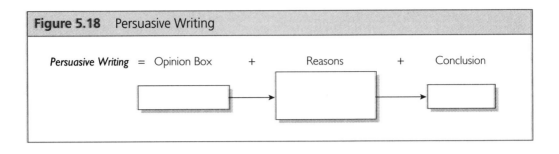

Figure 5.19   Top Hat Thinking

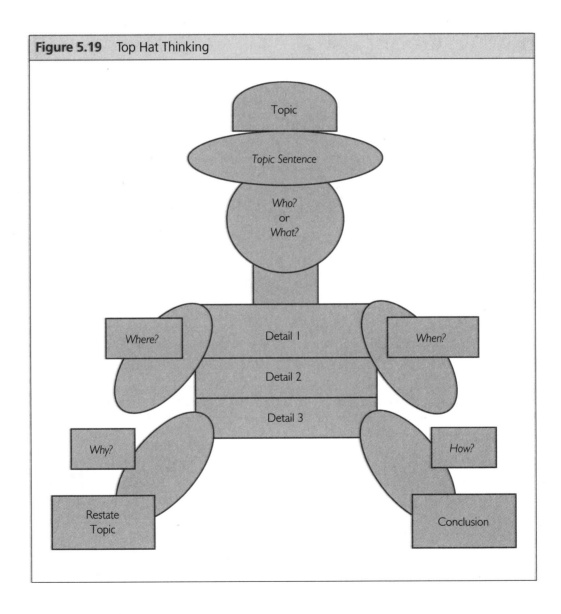

Stretch Your Main Ideas

The author can use the essay checklist in Figure 5.20 as a self-analysis tool during or after a revision or editing session.

Figure 5.20 Essay Checklist

Author _____ Date _____

ORGANIZATION

_____ My information is told in order.

_____ Each paragraph has a main idea and supporting details.

_____ I have a quality beginning, middle, and end.

CONTENT

_____ I have an important or interesting topic.

_____ Each sentence supports or explains the topic.

_____ The reader can follow the flow of thoughts.

SENTENCE STRUCTURE

_____ A variety of sentences is used.

_____ Each sentence expresses a complete thought.

_____ I use the best words to express my meaning.

DETAILS/MAIN IDEA

_____ All details tell about the subject.

_____ I have enough details to give needed information.

STYLE

_____ The writing form is consistent.

_____ Many words activate the readers' senses and stir emotions.

_____ Dialogue is used.

_____ Adjectives and adverbs create vivid mental pictures.

MECHANICS

_____ All sentences begin with a capital letter.

_____ The correct punctuation is used.

_____ Spelling errors are corrected.

_____ Paragraphs are indented.

_____ My work is neat and legible.

RHYMES AND RIDDLES

Students enjoy using content information to create rhymes and riddles. Relevant data, facts, and concepts are easily remembered when they are processed in these creative ways. Adapt the following structured forms and examples for young authors to use with content information.

Adapting Poetry

Limericks

Example

Five lines	My thoughts are written in black and white.
Lines 1, 2, and 5 rhyme.	On paper my ideas are quite a sight!
Lines 3 and 4 rhyme.	No one has thoughts just like mine.
	Words spill out of my head line by line.
	I am an author each time I write.

A–D Time

Example

Lines 1–4 begin with A–D.	Alligators glide through the sand.
	Birds dance on the water's edge.
	Crabs crawl over broken shells.
	Dragonflies flock at dusk.
Line 5 begins with any letter.	Nature's creatures take careless risks.

Ballad

Example

A ballad tells a story.	Did you know Davy Crockett?
It is written in four-line stanzas.	He fought with Texas against Mexico.
	He was a Tennessee volunteer.
Lines 2 and 4 rhyme.	He died at the Alamo.

Couplet

Example

A couplet has two lines that rhyme.	President Carter received the Nobel Peace Prize,
	For promoting world peace in our lives.

Haiku

The first line has five syllables.	Here, five syllables,
The second line has seven syllables.	Line two, seven syllables,
The third line has five syllables	Third line, again five.

One-to-One Diamond

This writing example is based on the diamante structure, which presents seven lines in the shape of a diamond. Select two nouns from the content that are opposites. The first noun is placed on the first line. The opposite noun is placed on the seventh line.

Line		Example
1	One noun	Peace
2	Two adjectives to describe #1	democratic, tranquil
3	Three action verbs	surrounds, calms, spreads
4	Two adjectives each to describe #1 and #7	quiet, serene, booming, bloody
5	Three action verbs	invades, scares, destroys
6	Two adjectives for the last noun	chemical, biological
7	One noun	War

Riddles

Riddles give hints to a specific answer. The statements are written as clues to solve a thought-provoking question or statement. Here are some examples.

I wore small glasses.

I was a patriot in the American Revolution.

I discovered electricity while flying a kite.

Who am I? _____

Answer: Benjamin Franklin

I am a famous dance form.

I am created with spins and other graceful movements.

The *Nutcracker*, a fantasy-filled Christmas story, is told with my moves.

Dancers must be on their toes to display my art form.

What am I? _____

Answer: Ballet

Poetry Adaptations for Content

Well-known poems provide patterns for creative use of content information. Teach students how to use the lines from various types of poetry to apply knowledge gained from the topic. Here are three examples.

**"Stopping by Woods on a
Snowy Evening" by Robert Frost**
Whose woods these are
I think I know.
His house is in the village though.

**Adaptation for
Problem Solving**
The answer here
I soon will know.
I just follow the steps as I go.

"Trees" by Joyce Kilmer
I think that I shall never see
A poem as lovely as a tree.

Adaptation for History
I think that I shall never see
A general as famous as Robert E. Lee.

"Fog" by Carl Sandburg
The fog comes on little cat feet.
It sits looking
Over harbor and city
On silent haunches
And then moves on.

"Icy Rain": Adaptation for Science
The sleet glides on big bear paws.
It starts pouring
Over glaciers and mountains
In stinging free falls,
Then slinks away.

GETTING TO KNOW TEXT CHARACTERS

*When children write stories, they imagine characters and construct themselves
as human beings at the same time.*
—Donald H. Graves (1999)

Use the following activities in all curriculum areas to explore famous people of yesterday or today in experiences related to fiction or nonfiction. The character strategies
are designed to showcase the students' knowledge. The students' knowledge and level
of success are reflected in their ability to adapt the information in their writing.

Content-Character Connections

1. Identify the characters studied.

2. Ask students to number off to match the number of characters. For example, if
   five characters are identified, the students number off with 1, 2, 3, 4, 5/1, 2, 3,
   4, 5. Continue to number off until all students have a number.

3. Learners who have number 1 form a group and work together. Learners who
   have number 2 form a group and work together. Continue forming groups.

4. Assign a character to each group.

5. Individual members gather the information for the assigned character and create related notes to share with the group.

6. The group compiles the individual data and decides what information will be
   reported and how to present it.

7. Each group member has a role in the presentation.

8. The group gathers props and artifacts.

9. The groups have time to rehearse the performances, present, and celebrate.

Encourage the audience to take notes, ask questions, and discuss each character with the information learned.

Showcasing a Famous Person

The following guide is used with students as they begin research experiences with important people in the topic of study.

1. Name of the person _____

2. List three personal attributes describing the individual.

   _____

3. This person is famous because _____.

4. This person impacts us today because _____.

5. Adjective _____, _____, _____

6. I liked _____ because _____.
   or
   I did not like _____ because _____.

7. I need to remember the following facts about this person: _____

   _____

Character Trace

1. Draw a large outline of the character studied.

2. Label and dress the character to illustrate the character's interests and personality. Include items that reflect the time period.

3. Display the character. Learn and enjoy!

Note: Teachers who have several classes may choose one character for a total class project.

Place a large sheet of butcher paper on the wall as a background for the characters to create a mural depicting the setting. Create competition between classes to make the assignment more challenging. These characters make excellent hall and door decor.

Famous Person Gala

1. Go on a scavenger hunt to find facts and trivia related to the assigned character. Write the gathered information on note cards.

2. Make a life-sized replica of the famous person or character studied.

3. Create outfits for the character from available items, scrap material, or clothes from home.

4. Stuff the clothing with newspaper or rags.

5. Surround the character with artifacts, music, and other information to portray his or her traits, experiences, and contributions.

6. Plan the most effective way to present the information.

7. Present the report in a unique way to reflect the person's importance and personality.

8. Tell the audience to take notes on each character.

9. Celebrate!

Characters in the Content Scene

This activity teaches students how to process information through creative writing. The teacher selects the genre for the writing activity. The students use a grid similar to the one presented in Figure 5.21 to create characters who interact with the content information. Give students the following directions:

1. Use a spinner or roll a die to select the character, the attribute, the time, his or her feelings, the place, and a companion.

2. Write a narrative about the selected character interacting with information you learned in the study. Be sure to use facts and details related to the topic.

Figure 5.21   Create a Character

	Character	Attributes	Time	Feelings	Place	Companion
1	elderly man	tall	long ago	scared	beach	friend
2	young lady	short	now	angry	mall	dog
3	toddler	adventurous	later	sad	park	teenager
4	baby	happy	tomorrow	afraid	woods	lion
5	young boy	sad	yesterday	sleepy	cave	partner
6	teenager	sneaky	earlier	happy	tent	sister

Example

Character and scene created: young lady, tall, yesterday, angry, park, friend

Selected Content: equivalent fractions

Genre: Narrative

<u>Yesterday</u> I saw a <u>tall</u> <u>young lady</u> jogging in the <u>park</u> with a <u>friend</u>. They stopped to rest and share a nutritious snack bar. As they broke it in half, a girl ran up to them to ask for directions to the exit. She appeared <u>angry</u> because she could not find her way out of the park.

They offered her a portion of their snack bar. Each friend broke her half of the bar into thirds, making a total of six pieces, and gave the girl two pieces. Each person had two-sixths or one-third of the snack. The ladies gave their new friend directions to the park exit. She waved good-bye with a smile on her face.

Character Spotlight

A screen script is a story written for a movie. It may be based on a true story or come from your imagination. Choose an interesting character and plot from the content lesson. Divide the story into three acts.

Act I

1. Introduce the characters.

2. Describe the main character in a way that will make the audience want to cheer.

3. Use an exciting action or event to grab the viewer's attention.

4. Create a problem or a struggle for the main character.

Act II

1. Present the character's attempts to overcome the struggle or problem.

2. Describe the character's attempt to solve the problem.

3. Present another conflict or problem as this act ends.

Act III

1. Explain the character's actions as the problems are solved.

2. Describe the character's return to a normal or happy life.

3. Ask each group to draw a stick figure on a piece of paper. See Figure 5.22, Reflections on a Stick, on page 116.)

4. Place three or four of the following terms around the stick figure for students to brainstorm in relation to the important person or character: *seeing, thinking, hearing, saying, strengths, touching, feelings, traveling,* and *weaknesses.*

Figure 5.22   Reflections on a Stick

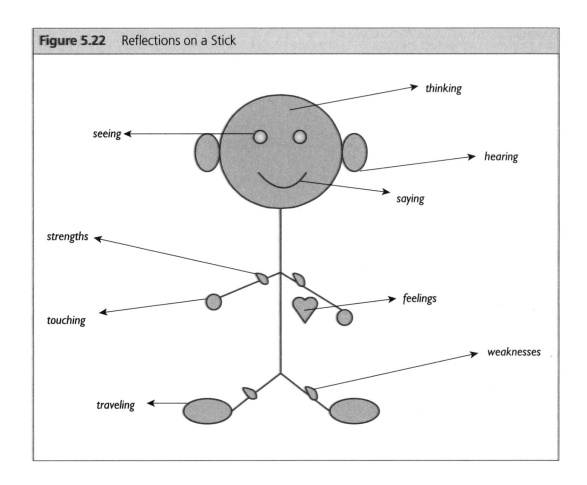

More Character Activities

- Create a song, riddle, jingle, rap, or cheer about a character's life.
- Log the events in the individual's life.
- Describe what it would have been like to live during the time of this person.
- Make a speech as the character.
- Create a choral reading to tell about his or her life.
- Write about the character as if you were a newspaper reporter or a critic.
- Develop a job description for the character.

Character Graphic Organizers

I. View a Character or Important Person

A. Draw a picture of an important person in a setting from the reading.

B. List character traits, attributes, or descriptors.

C. Name and explain the character's important contributions.

II. Compare Traits From the Text Evidence

A. Name two important people from the unit of study, a story, or novel. Select characters who have different opinions or views.

B. List the unique or different traits of each person.

C. Write evidence from the reading to prove that your information is correct. Include page numbers.

Person A _____	Page	Person B _____	Page
Trait _____ _____ _____		Trait _____ _____ _____	
Proof From Text	*Page*	*Proof From Text*	*Page*
_____ _____ _____		_____ _____ _____	
Why do you think they have these traits? How did these traits impact the story?			

III. Characterizations of an Important Person or Book Character

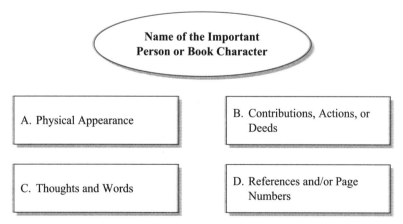

Caricature Creations

1. Draw a caricature of a famous person in the lesson or story character.
2. Place the setting around the caricature from the reading information.
3. Place an appropriate, informative caption under the picture.
4. Write information about the famous person or story character.

Name of the Famous Person or Story Character
_____

Caricature
Caption

Facts to remember about the person or character.

SEQUENCING WITH GRAPHIC ORGANIZERS

Use sequencing to place thoughts in order for prewriting. The content must flow logically. Often in writing activities, students brainstorm their ideas, and then the prewriting experience ends. Have students use organizers similar to the following to record their brainstormed thoughts.

From Thoughts to Priorities

1. Brainstorm ideas for stating one side of an issue. Identify a solution to a problem or steps in a procedure. Record the ideas in Box A. Do not worry about the order of this list.

2. In Box B, rank, prioritize, or sequence the brainstormed entries.

Problem or Topic _____

A. Brainstormed Ideas	B. Prioritized List
	1.
	2.
	3.

Chain of Events

1. Place events, procedures, steps to a problem, or stages in a sequence.

2. Use the numbered bubbles to write each item in the correct order.

3. Use a different color or font for each step or item to assist with memory of the order.

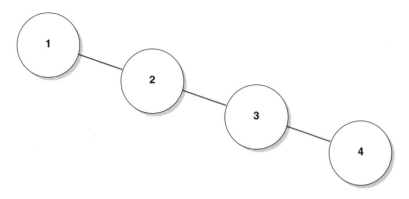

From Problems to Solutions

A. Problem

Who?	What?	When?	Where?	How?	Why?

B. Solutions

Attempted Solutions	Results
1.	1.
2.	2.
3.	3.

C. End Results: A Summary

Time Line

1. Place the significant dates of a period of study in sequential order on the left side of the vertical time line.

2. Under each date, write the name of the event.

3. On the right side of the time line, directly across from the date, add details to remember about the date and the event.

4. Add a summary or conclusion, as needed.

Date: Event:	Details:
Date: Event:	Details:
Date: Event:	Details:
Date: Event:	Details:
Summary or Conclusion:	

FORTY-THREE FROM A TO Z: WRITING ACTIVITIES

Students respond to new and unique activities. In *How the Brain Learns* (2006), David Sousa states that the brain has a "persistent interest in novelty" (p. 28); that is, to changes occurring in the environment. Unique experiences improve the brain's ability to store and to search for information. Plan to use a wide spectrum of innovative teaching and writing strategies to stay out of teaching ruts! Using novel content information generates excitement and enjoyment in the learning process. Variety is an effective motivational tool because it focuses attention and develops the learners, who eagerly look forward to writing activities.

The following activities are assigned to encourage reluctant writers and engage students with content information across the curriculum. They are designed to use before, during, or after content lessons. These differentiated experiences also provide opportunities for learners to grow as authors.

Alliteration

1. Choose a letter of the alphabet.

2. Brainstorm words with the same beginning sound.

3. Write alliterations related to the content information with the words that begin with the same sound.

Example

People pollute ponds pitching paper plates.

Brain Bash

1. Work in teams of three or four students.

2. List all possible responses to a question related to the topic of study.

3. Set a two- to three-minute time limit for brainstorming.

4. Choose one group member as the recorder to write the brainstormed list.

5. Praise the group with the longest accurate list.

6. Compile the responses, making a class list.

Examples

Name objects shaped like a rectangle.

What can be poured from a bottle?

List all of the flying animals you know.

Crack the Code

Write important facts in a special code or cipher. The simplest cipher uses letters of the alphabet in sequence, as shown below. Students enjoy creating challenging codes.

1	2	3	4	5	6	7	8	9	10	11	12	13	14	15	16	17	18	19	20	21	22	23	24	25	26
A	B	C	D	E	F	G	H	I	J	K	L	M	N	O	P	Q	R	S	T	U	V	W	X	Y	Z

Decipher the following message using the code above. Hyphens separate letters. Asterisks separate words.

23–18–9–20–9–14–7* 19–20–18–1–20–5–7–9–5–19* 3–1–14* 2–5* 21–19–5–4* 9–14*
1–12—12* 3–15–14–20–5–14–20* 1–18–5–1–19.

Answer: _____

Community Connections

Plan writing activities related to the unit of study to involve the community. Students can make personal connections with individuals, agencies, and groups in the local area through their writing experiences. Try these communication ideas:

- Write notes to veterans, politicians, or important leaders.
- Create place mats with special notes and poems for nursing homes.
- Invite a government official to share the role of writing on the job.
- Write a biography or tribute for an important individual, such as a local hero or role model. Plan a celebration to honor this person.
- Conduct environmental investigations and write possible solutions to the concerns.
- Write about the cultures of people represented in the community to honor diversity.
- Write an ad for your favorite restaurant.
- Create a blog listing public service opportunities for citizens.
- Write inviting ads for upcoming community events students can attend.

Dear Author

Write to the textbook author. This experience will focus students' attention on the value of the information in the text and develop letter-writing skills. Guide writers with the following statements and questions:

I like this textbook because _____.

You could improve this text by _____.

Why did you write about _____ in this chapter?

Why didn't you include _____?

I learned from you that _____.

It would help students if you _____in your next book.

The part I liked best in the book was _____.

Dreaming

Choose a topic, object, concept, or vocabulary word from the unit of study and write a metaphor about dreaming.

Examples

If I were the _____, I would _____.

If I were the <u>diameter</u>, I would feel strong because I could cross the center of a circle at any point and know that my line would cut the circle in half.

Egg on Your Face

"Egg on your face" is an expression used to describe deep embarrassment.

1. Think of a time when you had "egg on your face."

2. Describe the events leading to the embarrassment.

3. Explain exactly how you felt.

4. What advice would you give someone who has egg on his or her face?

Eyewitness Accounts

An eyewitness account is a report prepared by a person on the scene. It reveals everything viewed, heard, and felt. This activity provides practice with sequencing, organizing thoughts, and using vivid details to describe events or happenings.

Use this expository writing activity within units of study to show young authors how to make events, characters, and scenes vivid in the reader's mind. Tell the authors to record the information as if they are reporting in a live newscast.

Examples

Topic	Reporter
Pollination	Bee
A historic battle	Soldier
Oceanography	Shark
Measurement	Yardstick
Sports	Volleyball
Computer technology	Mouse

Fact Frames

Fact frames organize information in the unit of study using illustrations.

1. List the facts.

2. Identify the number of frames needed to illustrate the facts.

3. Draw one illustration for each fact frame.

4. Write or list the important facts in graffiti style around each picture.

5. Organize the fact frames in sequential order.

Fit as a Fiddle

The phrase "fit as a fiddle" means "in good health."

1. What would someone do to stay fit as a fiddle?

2. Describe what you would hear if someone played a fiddle that was "not fit."

3. Write a fit-as-a-fiddle rap.

Flip It

Make a flip book to record information. Use three sheets of paper. Follow these directions:

1. Crease and fold down one-fourth of the first sheet of paper.

2. Crease and fold down one-half of the second sheet of paper.

3. Crease and fold down three-fourths of the third sheet of paper.

4. Slide the folded end of the paper with one-half folded inside the fold of the paper with the one-fourth crease.

5. Slide the paper with the three-fourths crease folded inside the one-half fold.

6. Staple the papers together on the fold.

7. Write the title of the flip book on the top fold.

8. Write related information on other pages in the flip book.

Get It to Go!

Ask students to write questions from the unit of study with one-word answers. Tell students to write each question on a separate card with the answer on the back of the card. Use the cards in the following activity, which is effective with small groups or the total class.

Identify a student as the first Challenger. Arrange seats in a circle so the Challenger can move easily behind each participant's chair. Use these directions to guide the game.

1. Ask a question from the cards.

2. The seated student and the Challenger compete to be the one to "get it," or say the correct answer first.
   - If the seated student says the answer correctly before the Challenger, he or she takes the Challenger's place. The Challenger sits in the vacated chair.
   - If the Challenger answers correctly first, or if the seated student and the Challenger say the correct answer at the same time, the Challenger maintains the "to go" position and moves behind the next student's chair.
   - Each member of the class or group listens to questions and responses until the Challenger is standing behind his or her chair.

3. Each Challenger earns a point for each correct answer.

4. Celebrate with the "Get It to Go" winner.

Note: Simple word problems and content area facts can be written by students for a "Get It to Go" game.

Hitch Your Wagon to a Star

The expression "Hitch your wagon to a star" advises everyone to aim high and follow his or her dreams.

1. List your talents or strengths.

2. What are your dreams for the future?

3. How can you use your talents or strengths to "hitch" your dreams to a star?

4. What can you do to improve and use your talents and strengths?

If I Were in Your Shoes

Put yourself in the place of a character and try some of the following sentence starters:

- If I were as famous as _____, I would _____.

- If I were _____ and I could become invisible, I would _____.

- If I could spend the day with _____, I would _____.

In the Spotlight

Choose a person in the passage or unit of study to recognize or honor. Answer the following questions. Design a certificate, medal, badge, or plaque to honor the person in the spotlight.

- The star in my story is _____. Why? _____

- I want to honor _____ because _____.

- I can describe this person as being _____, _____, _____, and _____.

- If I could award _____with a special title, it would be _____.

Jump on the Bandwagon

"Jump on the bandwagon" is an expression used to ask someone to join an activity because other people are in it. The earliest bandwagons were pulled by horses. Bands played on the wagons to encourage people to join the people on the wagon in support of a particular person.

Answer the following questions:

- When is it a good idea to "jump on the bandwagon"? Why?

- When would it be dangerous to "jump on the bandwagon"? Why?

- What are some things friends might say to persuade you to join them on the "bandwagon"?

- Describe a time when you decided you should not "jump on a bandwagon."

Keepsakes

A keepsake is a special item you treasure and want to keep.

1. Create a list of your keepsakes.

2. What makes each keepsake a special treasure?

3. How did you receive your favorite keepsake?

Last Blast

Choose one of the following prompts. Write about the experience.

The last movie I saw _____.

The last time I ate in a restaurant _____.

The last time I visited with a friend, we _____.

The last time I went shopping, I _____.

The last time I had fun with a friend was when _____.

The last time I received a prized possession, I was _____.

The last time I felt excited was when _____._____

The last I giggled was _____.

Look Who's Talking

1. Write an imaginary conversation taking place between you and a character or an important person in the unit of study.

Example

Student:	"Hello, Columbus! How did you feel when you met the Native Americans?"
Columbus:	"Well, Billy, it was strange and exciting. I called the people Indians, because I thought I had reached India."

2. Choose two concepts from the unit of study. Assign each concept to a student. Tell each student to take on the role of the concept and talk to each other.

Example

Latitude and Longitude are having a conversation:

Longitude exclaims:	"Hey, Latitude! Look at me! All of my lines cross the equator, the hottest place on earth."
Latitude responds:	"Well, you don't have very much to brag about. My zero line is on the hot equator at all times. How tough do you think I have to be?"

3. Ask students to write a conversation with two animals, insects, objects, or people in the unit of study.

Examples

Mars and Jupiter	root and a stem	popcorn and soda
lightning and thunder	square and octagon	ball and bat
diameter and radius	nickel and a dollar	DVD player and movie

Mailbox

Designate a special container for student and teacher correspondence. Display directions and topic suggestions for writing the communications. Use the box for suggestions, questions, or notes. The teacher or other designated individual reads and answers the mail.

Musical Facts

Create a song with three to five facts in the study. Use a familiar tune so that the students do not struggle with the melody. When using this strategy, the emphasis is on learning the information.

Example

Fact or Opinion

(Tune: "Mary Had a Little Lamb")

A fact is the truth with evidence you know,

Evidence you know, evidence you know.

A fact is the truth with evidence you know.

So always search for the facts.

An opinion is a belief you can take or let go,

Take or let go, take or let go.

An opinion is a belief you can take or let go,

So choose your opinions wisely.

—Chapman and King

My Swaying Ways

Persuasion sways or changes beliefs. Give examples of persuasion that are meaningful to students and give them time to identify occasions when they have tried the technique. Choose a topic or issue directly affecting students.

Examples

Computer time	In-class movies
Snack machines in the cafeteria	Wearing uniforms in school
Hall passes	Longer school days
Selecting a new mascot design	More free play or breaks

Use following guidelines to teach persuasive writing skills:

1. Write your personal opinion on _____.

2. Survey others to find out how they feel about it. Gather their opinions to show that there is more than one side to the issue. Ask them to state their beliefs or points of view on the topic or issue.

3. Write your platform or beliefs. Explain why you have these beliefs.

4. Draw a conclusion stating your feelings or opinions.

5. Use your feelings and opinions to sway others to your side of the issue.

Needle in a Haystack

The phrase "It is like looking for a needle in a haystack," may be heard when a person is searching for a lost object.

Ask students if they have ever lost something that they could not find even after a long, thorough search. Tell them to write about how they felt as they were looking for the "needle in a haystack." Here are some prompts you may use:

- I lost a _____ in _____ several _____ago.
- My (friend, mother, brother) lost a _____. We looked _____.
- I felt _____when I lost _____.

Note Play

Take notes on newscasts, movies, favorite television shows, and documentaries to practice note taking. Get together with peers and discuss the most useful notes.

Choose one of the following areas to rewrite:

The dialogue   A character's role   The plot   The setting   The ending

Open Sesame!

The magic phrase "Open sesame!" was used by thieves in the story of Ali Baba in the *Arabian Nights*. They hid stolen treasures in a sealed cave. The entrance opened when they spoke the words "Open sesame!"

If these words opened special places for you, how and where would you use them? Write a story about the adventure you would have after you passed through the door.

Pictogram

Choose a shape from the unit of study. Create an outline for the shape using words, phrases, sentences, paragraphs, or poetry related to the topic.

Quiz Whiz

Write trivia questions related to the topic of study on individual index cards. Write the answers on the back of each card. Use the cards to create a game such as "Who Wants to Be a Millionaire?" or "Jeopardy."

Running on Empty

"Running on empty" is a phrase that relates to a very low level of gas in the tank of a vehicle. The driver wonders if he or she will reach the destination with the remaining fuel. This phrase is used by people who are tired and still have tasks they must complete.

Brainstorm experiences in which you ran out of energy but you had to keep going by "running on empty." Select one event and write a story about it. The following questions can be used to guide your prewriting thinking:

- Why did you select this experience?

- How did you feel at the beginning of the experience?

- What made you keep going when you had felt as though you were "running on empty"?

Smart Shirt

Design a T-shirt to detail a vocabulary word, a topic, an event, a region, a setting, or a person being studied.

Example

1. Write the selected word in the center of the shirt.

2. Write an adjective to describe the word directly below the word.

3. Write an attribute in the bottom right corner.

4. Write interesting trivia in the bottom left corner.

5. Write an example on one sleeve.

6. Illustrate the word on the other sleeve.

The Eyes Have It

Choose a place or thing. Personify it by giving an object nearby the "eyes" to see and describe the place or thing. Write the object's observations.

Examples

- A grain of sand describing the beach

- A wheel spoke describing a bicycle

- A net describing a basketball game

- A saddle describing a horse

- A book describing an author

This Is My Life

Time lines place events in sequential order using a scale of dates. They can be used to view the life of an individual or events in the unit of study.

Use the following activity to introduce time lines. Students enjoy sharing important events in their lives. Use a long strip of paper, such as adding machine tape. Ask students to create time lines to identify the highlights in their lives.

Example

0	5	7	14	17
Birth	Disneyland	Swimming Lesson	Soccer Trophy	Driver's License

Through My Eyes

Write a story in the first person to share a personal experience with one of the following:

On a skateboard	In your yard	On a trip	With a video game
While eating	During the night	On an adventure	While swimming

Triangle Tricks

Use Figure 5.17 in this activity.

1. Begin by selecting a word to fit in the boxes on the bottom row.

2. Drop one letter of the original word. Rearrange the letters to create a new word in the boxes above the original word.

3. Continue this procedure, making new words until you reach the box at the top of the triangle.

4. Write a story using the words in the triangles.

5. Try this triangle trick and then make up your own.

Up a Creek Without a Paddle

Ask students if they have ever been in so much trouble that they believed there was no way out of it. If they have had this experience, they have been "up a creek without a paddle."

1. What kind of trouble did you get into that left you "up a creek without a paddle"?

2. What did you do to try to get yourself out of trouble?

3. What did you learn from the event?

Figure 5.17   Triangle Tricks

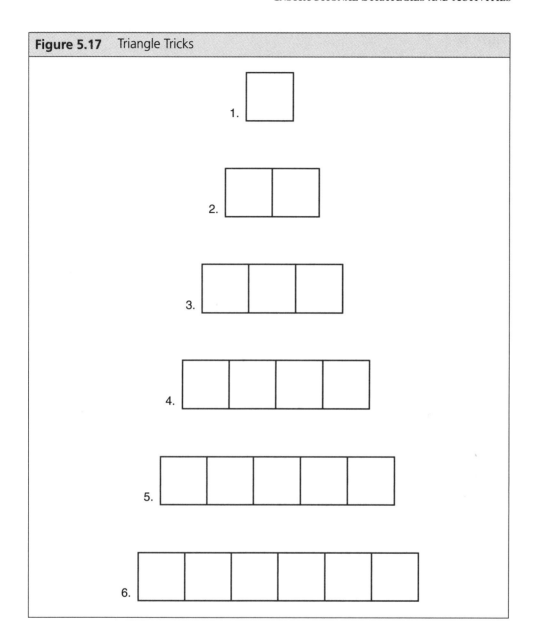

Upset the Applecart

Ask students if anyone or anything has ever interfered with their exciting activities or plans.

1. Describe an exciting plan or event that had to end because someone or something "upset your applecart."

2. How did you react to the accident or surprise that made your plans or activities change?

Vamoose

Vamoose is a slang term meaning "to leave a place quickly."

1. List places that gave you the feeling that you needed to vamoose, or leave.

2. Did you have to stay and deal with the vamoose feelings?

3. Explain how you feel when you have to be somewhere you don't want to be.

VIP

Pronounce each letter in *VIP*. This is an acronym for "very important person."

1. Describe a VIP you know.

2. What makes this person a VIP?

3. How are you a VIP for a friend, a pet, or a family member?

4. Draw a caricature of the VIP and label the attributes.

Vocabulary Predictions

The following activity is designed for students to write predictions by using vocabulary words in new content lessons. This exercise demonstrates the reading and writing connection. The teacher lists five to seven key words, names, and phrases from the upcoming study. Challenge students to use the key words and terms in a paragraph in the next unit of study.

Example

Vocabulary words: kangaroo, Australia, Ayers Rock, Great Barrier Reef

Student's prediction: We are going to study the continent of Australia. We will learn about the sea creatures in the Great Barrier Reef. I think we will find out why Ayers Rock is important. I bet we read about kangaroos. I hope we find out how long a baby kangaroo stays in the mother's pouch.

Walk on Eggshells

The phrase *walk on eggshells* means "to be very careful."

1. Think of a time when you had to "walk on eggshells," or be very careful about what you said to someone.

2. Describe the occasion.

3. When is it important to "walk on eggshells" while talking to someone?

4. Create a cartoon illustrating someone walking on eggshells.

Writing Olympics

Tell students they are going to have a race to see who can write the most words within a free writing time limit. Choose a topic for the writing Olympics. Set a timer. Direct the students to either create a list or write in complete sentences.

Give students the following directions:

1. Write about your topic during the two- to three-minute time limit.
2. Count the number of words you wrote.
3. Celebrate with the winners and share the writing.

Note: Increase the time limit with each writing Olympics activity.

X Out

This phrase means to mark out or delete by placing the letter *X* over a word, phrase, sentence, or object.

1. Write about an object or activity you would like to "X out" of your life.
2. Why is this object or activity part of your life now?
3. Why do you want to "X out" this object or activity?

Yum Yum

1. List foods you like to eat.
2. Choose your favorite food from the list.
3. Write everything you know about your favorite food.
4. Describe how and when you like to eat your favorite food.

Zone in Reflection

Use the following activity as students leave the classroom:

1. Place a plus sign or the words "Pluses of the Lesson" on the left side of the door facing. A minus sign or the words "Minuses of the Lesson" are placed on the right side of the door facing.
2. Students list the pluses of today's lesson on a sticky note.
3. They list the minuses of the lesson, if any, on a separate sticky note. Use different colored markers or sticky notes for the pluses and the minuses.
4. Ask students to place their notes on the proper door facing as they leave the learning zone. The "Zone in Reflection" becomes the ticket from the room.

SUMMARY

Teachers make a difference in the writing journey of each life they touch. Content teachers in the differentiated classroom plan their students' writing experiences with careful attention to individual needs. They develop, support, and inspire young authors, whose skills last a lifetime.

PLANNING, ASSESSING, AND EVALUATING WRITING 6

It is physically impossible to see what is going on inside cocoons, where the butterfly's vibrant colors and intricate designs develop.

It is physically impossible to see transformations in the author's mind, where writing skills and potential evolve.

LESSON PLANNING MODEL FOR WRITING IN THE CONTENT AREAS

Many decisions are made as a lesson is designed with writing activities. The lesson plan contains strategies and ideas to meet students' needs (a) before, (b) during, and (c) after the writing experiences. Consider the following questions and prompts when developing an effective writing lesson.

Before Writing

Topic

1. What is this group's background knowledge on this topic?

2. Which preassessment tools will I use?

3. How will I "hook" students into wanting to write?

Purpose of the Assignment

1. What is the purpose of this writing assignment?

2. Which standards, concepts, objectives, or skills do students need.

Genre

1. What genre will students use to complete this assignment?

2. Will the students choose their genres, or will I assign them?

Time and Materials

1. How much time is needed for the assignment?

   _____ in class   _____ out of class

2. What materials will be needed to differentiate the writing assignment?

3. The assignment will be used as (check all that apply):

_____ Grade   _____ Part of notes   _____ Journaling entry

_____ Review   _____ Topic folder   _____ Portfolio entry

_____ Feedback   _____ Assignment to turn in   _____ Research

_____ Brainstorming ideas   _____ Other _____

During Writing

Check all that apply: _____Total group _____Alone _____Partner ____Small group

Place the grouping scenarios for instruction in order. For example, if the lesson is introduced to the total class, they move into small groups to practice, and they complete the lesson sharing with a partner, the flexible grouping scenarios are recorded as T/S/P.

Grouping scenarios _____

Notes for grouping students: _____

Will revision be included?   ____Yes   ____ No   If yes, how? _____

Will editing be included?   ____Yes   ____ No   If yes, how? _____

Will the first draft go through all the steps and become a "neat sheet"? ___Yes ___No

After Writing
Feedback

Who provides student feedback? Check each space that applies:

_____ Self _____ Teacher _____ Partner _____ Small group

The feedback will be presented in the form of

_____ a conference _____ written comments _____ a rubric

Publishing

Will the writing be shared? _____

If so, how? _____

Will the assignment be published in a specific format or sequence?

_____Yes ____ No If yes, how? _____

Will the work be displayed? _____Yes _____No

How? _____ Where? _____ Who? _____ (Students or Teacher) _____

EFFECTIVE ASSESSMENT TOOLS

Effective assessment tools identify the writer's strengths and weaknesses. For example, analyze many fiction and informational text writing samples, such as tests, journal entries, portfolio samples, and daily writing assignments. Remember, writing develops as an ongoing process over time. Each student takes ownership of writing develops as skills at a different rate, so it is important use the most effective assessment tool to gather the data needed to guide differentiated instruction.

Select, adapt, and design writing assessment tools to produce data that will enhance each student's growth as an author. Use a combination of formal and informal assessment tools to obtain the accurate picture of the writer's skills. Train students to use assessment tools to analyze their own strengths and weaknesses. Encourage students to be kind, constructive peer evaluators.

Informal Writing Assessment Tools
Examples

observations	cooperative writing	exit response tickets
station work	conversations	computer entries
notes	board work	bell ringer activity

Formal Writing Assessment Tools
Examples

portfolio samples	analysis of testing data	prewriting exercises
test answers	rubrics	writing samples
checklists	open-ended questions	informational writing
multiple choice	graphic organizers	fill in the blank

Prepare for Assessment Scenes

Writing is used extensively in the formal assessment scenes. Written responses to open-ended questions are required on standardized tests. The student must know how to use the basic steps of the writing process to organize ideas, draft, revise, and edit. Most writing tests emphasize content, organization, and style. A schoolwide emphasis on these three areas will increase scores. Students need to realize that writing on a topic consists of placing their talk or thoughts on paper. They must know enough about the topic to discuss it.

Use a prewriting activity to give learners an opportunity to organize their thoughts around the topic. Tell the students to use the same order of ideas they would use to tell someone about the topic. These notes and thoughts are used to write the paper. When a passage is written as it would be said orally, the content will be organized in the same order as the thoughts flow. The passage usually has style when the author writes as if he or she were talking.

When learners know how to recall and apply writing strategies automatically, they are able to showcase their skills. Figures 6.1, 6.2, 6.3, and 6.4 illustrate suggestions, forms, and ideas to adapt for the classroom. The observation checklist in Figure 6.4 is a flexible, practical tool designed to monitor specific skills and strategies. Use the examples and modify them as needed to observe, monitor, and score writing.

Figure 6.1 Class Writing Checklist

	Frequently	+
	Occasionally	O
Teacher _____	Seldom	S
Class _____ Date _____	Not Noted	N

Note: List the skills to observe and assess in the writing assignment in each section. The list will vary according to the class, the skills emphasized, and the content.

Student Name	Selection Title	Skills	Comments
1.			
2.			

Figure 6.2 Essay Analysis

Student _____

Essay Title _____ Date _____

Rater: ☐ Self   ☐ Teacher   ☐ Peer   ☐ Small Group

	Yes	No	Partial	Comments
1. Selection of subject				
2. Clear content				
3. Ideas organized				
4. Message conveyed				
5. Details used				
6. Voice/tense consistent				
7. Creativity evidenced				

Rubric for Scoring Essays

A *rubric* is an evaluation tool developed with specific criteria. The criteria reflect the expectations for a product, such as a project, a report, or a presentation. The levels are used to score the writer on a particular piece of work. The levels indicate the amount of assistance to provide for the student. Writers need to know and understand the rubric used to evaluate their work. Figure 6.5 on page 140 is a sample rubric for assessing essays.

Figure 6.3 Individual Writing Evaluation				
Name: _____				
Writing Selection: _____ Date: _____				
Rater: ❏ Self ❏ Teacher ❏ Peer ❏ Small Group				
Writing Area	*Fair*	*Good*	*Excellent*	*Comments*
Content *Contains significant information.*				
Organization *Develops content in sequence.*				
Focus *Sticks to the topic.*				
Mechanics *Uses correct spelling and punctuation.*				
Other				

NOTE: Each item on the above checklist can be weighted according to your state assessment requirements.

Figure 6.4 Observation Checklist				
Date _____ Class _____				
Note: List items to be observed in the column heads.				
Key: + Often * Occasionally → Trying				
Student Names	*Observable Traits*			*Comments*
1.				
2.				

Adapt the following guidelines when you use rubrics to assess student work:

- Vary the terms used in rubrics to create student-friendly evaluations. Students will enjoy using the following terms to add novelty to their self-evaluation writing scales.

○ Needs help	○ Improving	○ Good work	○ Great work
○ Emerging	○ Developing	○ Proficient	○ Exemplary
○ Crawling	○ Walking	○ Skipping	○ Running
○ Tasting	○ Sipping	○ Drinking	○ Guzzling

- Challenge students to create rubrics for their writing self-evaluations.

Figure 6.5 Essay Rubric	
Student _____ Date _____ Title of Writing Selection _____	*Scorer* ☐ Self ☐ Peer ☐ Teacher

5 Superior

Used clear, descriptive sentences and paragraphs.

Organized ideas.

Included important, concise information.

Used correct mechanics.

Captured the audience's attention.

4 Beyond Expectations

Wrote with descriptive sentences.

Used correct mechanics.

Created interest for the audience.

3 Acceptable

Wrote complete sentences.

Used basic mechanics.

Held the reader's interest to some extent.

2 Some Improvement Evident

Used a few complete sentences.

Included some correct punctuation and capitalization.

Shows some evidence of organization.

Low interest level shown.

I Needs Improvement

Used incomplete sentences.

Applied incorrect punctuation and capitalization.

Beginning, middle, and end are unclear.

Work is uninteresting to the audience.

Overall Score _____

Scales for Scoring Writing Assessments

Likert scales are often used as rating tools. The numbers applied are 1 through 10. We begin the following scales with the number 2. When students are present and participating, they deserve more than a 0 or 1. Design or use scales similar to the one in Figure 6.6 as easy-to-use self-assessment tools for students.

The assessment tool in Figure 6.7 is designed to evaluate a writing selection. It can be used by the author for self-checking, teacher feedback, or peer and small-group evaluation activities.

Figure 6.6   Self-Assessment Using Likert Scales

1. The content is on-topic.

   2 _____ 4 _____ 6 _____ 8

2. My writing is organized with a logical flow of ideas.

   2 _____ 4 _____ 6 _____ 8

3. My work contains accurate information.

   2 _____ 4 _____ 6 _____ 8

4. The passage shows my feelings and style as the author.

   2 _____ 4 _____ 6 _____ 8

5. This is one of my "Best Works."

   2 _____ 4 _____ 6 _____ 8

Figure 6.7   Evaluation Form for a Writing Selection

Author's Name: _____   **Date:** _____

Title of the Writing Selection: _____

Scorer: ☐   Self   ☐   Teacher   ☐   Peer   ☐   Small Group

1. Topic presented _____

2. Hook(s) _____

3. Supporting details _____

4. Examples provided _____

5. Value to the audience   5   4   3   2   1

6. Creativity   5   4   3   2   1

7. Closing _____   _____

8. Strengths _____   _____

9. Areas for improvement _____

10. Content/Organization

       Subject/Title   5   4   3   2   1

       Introduction   5   4   3   2   1

       Sequence   5   4   3   2   1

       Details   5   4   3   2   1

       Ending   5   4   3   2   1

11. Mechanics

       Punctuation   5   4   3   2   1

       Capitalization   5   4   3   2   1

       Spelling   5   4   3   2   1

12. Summary comments _____

The chart in Figure 6.8 can be used to identify errors in writing samples. When an area is cited as a weakness, teach the identified skill and then look for the correct application of the skill in future writing samples.

Figure 6.8   Revising and Editing Reference Chart

Areas of Importance	Common Writing Errors
1. Organization	Information is grouped illogically. Transitions are used incorrectly. Ideas do not flow logically. Ideas or events are not in the correct order.
2. Content	Information is not related to the assigned topic. Details do not support the main idea. Birdwalking, or straying from the topic, is evident.
3. Style	Is not written in a conversational style. Uses short, choppy sentences. Lacks descriptive words and phrases.
4. Sentence Structure	Uses fragments. Uses run-on sentences. Uses comma splices.
5. Mechanical	Uses incorrect spelling. Shows lack of capitalization skills. Has missing or incorrect punctuation.
6. Grammatical	Tense shifts incorrectly. Subjects and verbs are not in agreement. Pronoun references are unclear. Words are omitted.
7. Word Usage	Words chosen are not the most appropriate.

Project Rubric

Provide students with the project rubric for assessment when the project is assigned. Place the rubric in a packet including a time line so they will know when to expect checkpoints or conferences during and after the work. Allow everyone to select a project buddy to confer and meet with during the entire process. Include additional tasks and requirements to the time line for an extended project assignment. Create checkpoints along the way for students and the teacher to monitor project tasks. When time lines are followed, procrastinators learn the importance of ongoing work task segments, instead of putting off the work until the last couple of days before the due date. Figure 6.9 contains an example of a project time line, and Figure 6.10 presents a project rubric.

Figure 6.9	Project Partner Time Line	
Date	*Individual Tasks*	*Project Partner Tasks*
Visit 1 ———	❏ Write the goals for your project. ❏ Bring notes gathered on your topic.	❏ Take turns sharing your goals. ❏ Share your notes.
Visit 2 ———	❏ Bring two completed reference cards.	❏ Check your partner's work. ❏ Look for correct formatting and usage. ❏ Check the information to see that it is written in your partner's words, not the author's. ❏ Give recommendations, including how and where to use the information.
Visit 3 ———	❏ Bring your latest findings. ❏ Identify questions, problems, or concerns related to the project.	❏ Take turns sharing your new notes. Discuss the questions, comments, and concerns. ❏ Make a list of your needs and turn them in to the teacher, requesting assistance for the partner team, a private conference, or class discussion.
Visit 4 ———	❏ Bring in an artifact to use in your display.	❏ Share and discuss the displayed items for each project. ❏ Give an overview of plans for other items on the display. ❏ Share improvement ideas.with your partner.
———	❏ Bring in a rough draft of the research paper.	❏ Read and explain how you have met your goal. ❏ Write the facts you learned.
———	❏ Bring a picture or sketch of the display you are planning.	❏ Share ideas to improve the displays. ❏ Take notes.
Visit 5 ———	❏ Bring in notes and ideas for presenting your project.	❏ Go over the presentation plans. ❏ Discuss improvement ideas. ❏ Take notes.
Visit 6 ———	❏ Take a gallery walk to view each display. ❏ Take brief notes on each item.	❏ Take a gallery walk with your Project Partner. ❏ Discuss each display, note cards, and research papers. ❏ Combine and summarize your notes. ❏ Write what you learned from the presentations and the gallery walk. ❏ Share comments and questions.
Visit 7 ———	❏ Write your feelings about the project after everything is completed and turned in.	❏ Discuss and share what you have learned from the project, your partner, and others in the experience. ❏ Write reflective comments.
Visit 8 ———	❏ Evaluate your Project Partner ❏ Analyze the impact of the task-sharing process.	❏ Discuss what worked and what did not work for you. Identify the pluses and minuses of the tasks. ❏ Identify the parts of the procedure that need to be used in the next project assignment. ❏ Identify procedures or tasks that need to be omitted in the next assignment.

Figure 6.10   Project Rubric

Student: _____   Date: _____

Project Assignment: _____

Rater: _____ Self   _____ Peer _____ Teacher

Accuracy of Information

| 2 | 4 | 6 | 8 |

Comments

Research Gathered

| 2 | 4 | 6 | 8 |

Comments

Time Line Followed

| 2 | 4 | 6 | 8 |

Comments

Presentation Debut

| 2 | 4 | 6 | 8 |

Comments

Overall Project

| 2 | 4 | 6 | 8 |

Comments

Other:

Assessor	Student
Assessor's Signature _____	Student's Signature _____
Date _____	Date _____

Portfolios

A *content portfolio* is a special place to save work samples in a unit of focus. The materials chosen show evidence of the learner's progress, strengths, and needs.

Provide each student with a file or accordion folder to use as a subject area portfolio. Give students time to decorate the cover to represent the unit of study. Let each learner personalize the portfolio decor with bright and bold colors, and unique fonts. The designs make each portfolio easy to recognize and save time when they are distributed. In addition, you may use the following suggestions for the portfolio work:

- Designate a page to create a list of the portfolio's content with the entry date for each item. Place the same title and date on the piece of work.

- Create a skill list with space for additions. The teacher or the student may add new skills to the list as they are applied and learned. The student marks the skills that need more work. The list serves as a reminder for future attention and practice.

- Identify space for a brainstorming list. Keep the list of ideas to use later.

- Work samples represent the student's "Best Work" because the portfolio it reflects the learner's abilities and performances.

Portfolio Reflections

The comments in Figure 6.11 can be placed on a portfolio selection as a reflection task. Students can place a reflection statement on a sticky note and attach it to the work.

Figure 6.11   Portfolio Reflection Comments

- I decided to write this piece because _____.

- I took a risk by_____.

- I learned _____.

- This was like an experiment because _____.

- The next time I write, I will _____.

- This is a good piece of writing because _____.

Portfolio Conferences

A portfolio conference guide assists the listening partner as entries are analyzed and discussed. The partners make suggestions, find possible problems, and develop workable solutions together. The partner is an effective listener and lets the author lead the discussion. A listening partner uses statements or questions such as the following to plan and use in a portfolio conference:

- Tell me about this selection.
- What part did you like best?
- I like the _____.
- Do you have enough information?
- Why did you choose this topic?
- How does this writing compare to other pieces you have written?
- This part is not clear to me. Will you explain it?
- What could you do to make this work better?
- Does the beginning grab the reader's attention?
- Are you happy with the beginning/the ending?
- Is your paper in the right order?
- What do you need to add or delete?
- Did you stick to the topic throughout your writing?
- Others _____

The student needs time to complete a portfolio conference form before a partner discussion session begins. The student can use the sample report form in Figure 6.12 as a guide for leading a portfolio conference with a peer.

Grading a Writing Piece

When teachers assess student writing, they must deal with questions unique to evaluating student work in this form. How do you grade open-ended questions? Do you grade the learner's current writing skills or is the grade based on improvements?

Formal writing tests usually give more weight to the content of a passage and less weight to mechanics. The administrators and faculty need to come to consensus on the writing areas to emphasize throughout the school, if specific requirements are not available from the state and local entities.

Figure 6.12   Portfolio Conference Guide

1. Personal Identification Data

Student: _____   Class Period: _____

Date of Gathering: From _____ to _____

Unit/Topic: _____   Teacher: _____

2. Table of Contents Entries: List each work sample in the portfolio's table of contents. Use the title of the work and the date it was completed. Students identify each entry as either completed or as work in progress.

3. Place two lines or boxes at the end of each entry on the list. The first box is checked when the partner sees the work. The second box is checked when the discussion is completed.

EXAMPLE

   (a) Editorial Cartoon   Completed 5/14   ☐   ☐   ☐

   (b) Journal Entry   Completed 5/17   ☐   ☐   ☐

Note: Specific entries for discussion are assigned by the teacher or chosen by the student.

---

4. Provide a comment section for the portfolio conference.

EXAMPLE

What did you learn from the conference?

Author: _____

Partner: _____

---

5. The signature section is provided so partners take responsibility for following conference procedures and staying on-task.

EXAMPLE

Author's Signature _____ Date _____

Partner's Signature _____ Date _____

SUMMARY

In a differentiated classroom, the teacher proactively plans and carries out varied approaches to content, process, and product in anticipation of and response to student differences in readiness, interest, and learning needs.

—Carol Ann Tomlinson (2001)

A goal of teachers is to provide the guidance and support each student needs to become a productive writer. Differentiated instruction across the content areas (see Figure 6.13) provides student authors with an understanding of their thinking styles, intelligences, and personality profiles. Recognition of the learner's strengths and genuine praise builds the young author's confidence in his or her writing ability. The learner views errors and weaknesses as opportunities to improve.

An effective author knows how to identify topics of interest and the most comfortable styles for formal and informal writing. The student knows how to use his or her knowledge and related experiences in writing. The productive young writer knows how to use various writing forms to communicate information learned. The student possesses a repertoire of writing strategies and can apply them automatically to organize and communicate ideas. The author knows the content must be presented clearly and keep the reader's attention, so the editor's input is valued.

The successful writer knows how to use the steps in the writing process and realizes that revisions are always possible. The learner is aware that there may be many revisions before the final copy is produced. The young author's pride is evident in the collection of notes, drafts, and final copies.

Internal motivation drives the author to succeed. The writer anticipates the rewards that come from audience appreciation and self-satisfaction. The author looks forward to each experience as a self-fulfilling challenge.

The Rest of the Story . . .

Metamorphosis of Butterflies and Writers

When entering a flower garden, a visitor sees more butterflies when moving slowly and quietly while looking carefully for the still, camouflaged creatures.

In the classroom, a teacher realizes the writing potential in young authors when carefully and patiently observing and identifying the learners' various skills and abilities.

The release of butterflies brings delight to the beholder as the beautiful creatures spread their wings and take their individual flights.

When teachers develop effective authors, they know the students have communicating tools for their individual writing journeys.

Remember!

Everyone is a writing teacher.
All students are writers.

Always

Build confidence.
Nurture uniqueness.
Cultivate writing destinies.

Figure 6.13   Writing Across the Content Areas

	Language Arts	Social Studies	Math	Science	Visual Arts	Vocational Studies	Physical Education and Health
Uses of Writing	Journals	Data gathering	Using data	Applying data	Journals	Lists	Rules
	Diaries	Research	Summaries	Charts	Critiques	Directions	Notes
	Critiques	Notes	Conclusions	Graphs	Summaries	Inventions	Posters
	Summaries	Interviews	Word problems	Interviews	Explanations	Interpretations	Brochures
	Procedures	Graphs	Procedures	Songs	Directions	Explanations	Captions
	Brainstorming	Map labels	Time lines	Experiments	Playbills	Procedures	Cheers
	Manuals	Statistics	Charts	Notes	Songs	Instructions	Instructions
	Ads	Time lines	Class notes	Observations	Poems	Portfolios	Diagrams
	Research	Reports	Labels	Logs Reports	Interpretations	Opinions	Charts
	Note cards	Labels	Graphs	Definitions	Research	Manuals	Signs
	Outlines	Charts	Diagrams	Statistics	Manuals	Labels	Plays
	Reports	Notes	Directions	Opinions	Diaries	Reports	Outlines
	Interviews	Descriptions	Definitions	Hypotheses	Logs	Summaries	Tips
	Analysis	Diaries	Reports	Theories	Materials	Conclusions	Definitions
	Opinions	Poems	Journals	Captions	Lists	Notes	Guides
		Songs	Research	Procedures	Plays	Captions	Handbooks

(Continued)

149

Figure 6.13 (Continued)

Uses of Writing	Language Arts	Social Studies	Math	Science	Visual Arts	Vocational Studies	Physical Education and Health
	Songs	Ads	Conclusions	Summaries	Invitations	E-mails	Biographies
	Jingles	Historical records	Rules	Editorials	Editorials	Charts	Creating plans
	Cheers	References	Formulas	Poems	Conclusions	Recipes	Analyses
	Raps	Lists	Guidelines	Lists	E-mails	Interviews	Diagnoses
	Comparisons	Logs	Progress reports	Labels	Designs	Designs	Applications
	Charts	E-mails	Self-evaluations	Research	Creations	Brainstorming	Agreements
	Graphs	Brainstorming	Statistics	Inventions	Inventions	Rules	Contracts
	Poems	History	Comparisons	Graphic organizers	Charts	Charts	Game reviews
	Interpretations	Reflections	Brainstorming	Problems	Graphic organizers	Lists	Medical reports
	Statistics	Graphic organizers	Analyses	Procedures	Signs	Reflections	Game highlights
	Observations	Biographies	Reflections	Diagnoses	Notes	Evaluations	Newspaper articles
	Notes	Time Lines	Notes	Contrasts	Articles	How-to Guides	First aid directions
	Reflections			Comparisons	Portfolios	Advertisements	Promotions
	Editorials				Captions	Research	Game statistics
	Letters						
	E-mails						
	Newsflashes						

APPENDIX

Category	Page	Not Yet	Some	Often	Usually
Chapter 1: Introduction	1				
Chapter 2: Establishing the Effective Writing Climate	9				
Instill Self-efficacy	9				
Develop Internal Motivation	10				
Develop Self-Regulated Learners	10				
Assessing the Affective Writing Climate	11				
Razzamatazz to Thingamajigs	13				
Cool Tools	13				
Material Magic	13				
Make the Size Fit	14				
Burrito Fold	14				
Accordion Fold	15				
Hotdog Fold	15				
High/Low Fold	15				
The Shape of Things	15				
Quarter Tear	16				
Paper Stripping	16				
Sticky Tabbing	16				
Rainbow Writing	17				
Ready References	17				

(Continued)

(Continued)

Category	Page	Not Yet	Some	Often	Usually
Chapter 4: Differentiating the Writing Process and Flexible Grouping	37				
Types of Writing	37				
Descriptive Writing	37				
Expository Writing	38				
Persuasive Writing	38				
Narrative Writing	40				
The Block Party	41				
The Writing Process	45				
Step 1: Getting Started: Prewriting	46				
Step 2: Sloppy Copy: First Draft	50				
Step 3: Hamming it Up: Revision	56				
Step 4: Tuning it Up: Editing	64				
Step 5: Neat Sheet: Final Copy	69				
Step 6: Sharing and Celebrating: Publishing	69				
Flexible Grouping	72				
T.A.P.S.	73				
T: Total Group	74				
A: Alone	74				
P: Partner	74				
S: Small Group	75				
Chapter 5: Instructional Strategies and Activities for the Differentiated Writing Classroom	77				
Teach Each Writing Strategy Strategically	77				
Informational Text Writing and Critical Thinking	77				
Writing Strategies for English Language Learners	79				

(Continued)

(Continued)

Category	Page	Not Yet	Some	Often	Usually
Differentiating Writing With Formats and Genres	80				
Using Personification to Process	84				
Planning For Individual Needs	85				
Choice Boards	85				
Agendas	88				
Individualized Writing Projects	88				
Language Experience Activities	88				
Writing Strategies	91				
Brainstorming	91				
Journaling	94				
Gathering Research	97				
Proposals and Contracts for Research	97				
Teacher's Role in Research	98				
Student's Role in Research	99				
Ways to Research a Topic	99				
Presenting Research Reports With "Zippidy-Do"	99				
Research Conferences	99				
Note Taking	101				
Note-Taking Tips for Listening	101				
Note-Taking Tips for Reading	102				
Tips for Creating Research Note Cards	102				
"On Line" With Outlines	103				
Rubrics	104				
Writing Essays	105				
Prewriting for Organizing Essays	105				
Rhymes and Riddles	110				
Getting to Know Text Characters	112				
Content-Character Connections	112				
Showcasing a Famous Person	113				

Category	Page	Not Yet	Some	Often	Usually
Character Trace	113				
Famous Person Gala	114				
Characters in the Content Scene	114				
Character Spotlight	115				
Reflections on a Stick	116				
Character Graphic Organizers	116				
Sequencing With Graphic Organizers	118				
From Thoughts to Priorities	118				
Chain of Events	118				
From Problems to Solutions	119				
Time Line	120				
Forty-three From A to Z	120				
Alliteration	121				
Brain Bash	121				
Crack the Code	121				
Community Connections	122				
Dear Author	122				
Dreaming	122				
Egg on Your Face	123				
Eyewitness Accounts	123				
Fact Frames	123				
Fit as a Fiddle	123				
Flip It	124				
Get it to Go!	124				
Hitch Your Wagon to a Star	125				
If I Were in Your Shoes	125				
In the Spotlight	125				
Jump on the Bandwagon	125				
Keepsakes	125				

(Continued)

(Continued)

Category	Page	Not Yet	Some	Often	Usually
Last Blast	126				
Look Who's Talking	126				
Mailbox	127				
Musical Facts	127				
My Swaying Ways	127				
Needle in a Haystack	128				
Note Play	128				
Open Sesame!	128				
Pictogram	128				
Quiz Whiz	128				
Running on Empty	129				
Smart Shirt	129				
The Eyes Have It	129				
This Is My Life	130				
Through My Eyes	130				
Triangle Tricks	130				
Up the Creek Without a Paddle	130				
Upset the Applecart	131				
Vamoose	132				
VIP	132				
Vocabulary Predictions	132				
Walk on Eggshells	132				
Writing Olympics	132				
X Out	133				
Yum! Yum!	133				
Zone in Reflection	133				

Category	Page	Not Yet	Some	Often	Usually
Chapter 6: Planning, Assessing, and Evaluating Writing	135				
Informal Writing Assessment Tools	137				
Formal Writing Assessment Tools	137				
Prepare for Assessment Scenes	137				
Class Writing Checklist	138				
Essay Analysis	138				
Self-Assessment Using Likert Scales	141				
Evaluation Form for a Writing Selection	141				
Revising and Editing Reference Chart	142				
Project Partner Time Line	143				
Project Rubric	144				
Portfolios	145				
Grading a Writing Piece	146				
Writing Across the Content Areas	149				

Our best wishes to you in giving your students the joy of writing and their wings as authors!

REFERENCES

Atwell, N. (1998). *In the middle: New understanding about writing, reading, and learning.* Portsmouth, NH: Heinemann.

Barone, D. M., & Taylor, J. (2006). *Improving students' writing, K–8.* Thousand Oaks, CA: Corwin.

Calkins, L. M. (1994). *The art of teaching writing.* Portsmouth, NH: Heinemann.

Chapman, C., & King, R. (2008). *Differentiated instructional management: Work smarter, not harder.* Thousand Oaks, CA: Corwin.

Chapman, C., & King, R. (2009). *Differentiated instructional strategies for reading in the content areas* (2nd ed.). Thousand Oaks, CA: Corwin.

Costa, A. L., & Kallick, B. (Eds.). (2000). *Activating and engaging habits of mind.* Alexandria, VA: Association for Supervision and Curriculum Development.

Cox, C. (2008). *Teaching language arts: A student-centered classroom* (6th ed.). Boston: Pearson/Allyn & Bacon.

Csikszentmihalyi, M. (1990). *Flow.* New York: Harper and Row.

Fisher, D., & Frey, N. (2007). *Checking for understanding: Formative assessment techniques for your classroom.* Alexandria, VA: Association for Supervision and Curriculum Development.

Frank, M. (1995). *If you're trying to teach kids how to write . . . You've gotta have this book.* Nashville, TN: Incentive.

Frost, R. (1939). The figure poem makes. In R. Frost, *Collected poems of Robert Frost* (new ed.). New York: Holt, Rinehart, and Winston.

Gardner, H. (1983). *Frames of mind: The theory of multiple intelligences.* New York: Basic Books.

Graves, D. (1983). *Writing: Teachers and children at work.* Portsmouth, NH: Heinemann.

Graves, D. (1999). *Bring life into learning: Create a lasting literacy.* Portsmouth, NH: Heinemann.

Gregory, G., & Chapman, C. (2006). *Differentiated instructional strategies: One size doesn't fit all* (2nd ed.). Thousand Oaks, CA: Corwin.

Hemingway, E. (1963). Interview With George Plimpton. In Van Wyck Brooks (Ed.), *Writers at work: The* Paris Review *interviews, second series* (pp. 217–239). New York: Viking.

Langer, J. A., & Applebee, A. N. (1987). *How writing shapes thinking: A study of teaching and learning* (NCTE Research Report No. 22). Urbana, IL: National Council of Teachers of English.

National Commission on Writing. (2003). *The neglected "R": The need for a writing revolution.* New York: College Entrance Examination Board.

Nessel, D. D., & Dixon, C. N. (2008). *Using the language experience approach with English language learners: Strategies for engaging students and developing literacy.* Thousand Oaks, CA: Corwin.

Reyes, S. A., & Vallone, T. L. (2008). *Constructivist strategies for teaching English language learners.* Thousand Oaks, CA: Corwin.

Santrock, J. W. (2009). *Educational psychology* (4th ed.). New York: McGraw-Hill.

Schmoker, M. (2007). Reading, writing, and thinking for all. *Educational Leadership, 64*(7), 63–66.

Siegler, R. S. (2004). *Children's thinking* (4th ed.). Upper Saddle River, NJ: Prentice Hall.

Sousa, D. (2006). *How the brain learns* (3rd ed.). Thousand Oaks, CA: Corwin.

Sternberg, R. J., & Grigorenko, E. (2007). *Teaching for successful intelligence: To increase student learning and achievement* (2nd ed.). Thousand Oaks, CA: Corwin.

Stipek, D. J. (1996). Motivation and instruction. In D. C. Berliner & R. C. Calfee (Eds.), *Handbook of educational psychology* (pp. 85–113). New York: Macmillan.

Tolstoy, L. (1969). In A. B. Goldenveizer, *Talks With Tolstoy* (S. S. Koteliansky & V. Woolf, Trans.). New York: Horizon Press. (Original work published 1923)

Tomlinson. (2001). Carol Ann Tomlinson, C. A. (2001). *Fulfilling the promise of the differentiated classroom: Strategies and tools for responsive teaching.* Alexandria, VA: Association for Supervision and Curriculum Development.]

Waugh, E. (1976). Irregular notes. In M. Davie (Ed.), *The diaries of Evelyn Waugh.* Boston Little Brown. (Diary entry dated December 25, 1962)

Willingham, D. T. (2006, Spring). How knowledge helps: It speeds and strengthens reading comprehension, learning—and thinking. *American Educator, 30,* 1–12. Retrieved December 31, 2008, from http://www.aft.org/pubs-reports/american_educator/issues/spring06/willingham.htm

INDEX

CORWIN
A SAGE Company

The Corwin logo—a raven striding across an open book—represents the union of courage and learning. Corwin is committed to improving education for all learners by publishing books and other professional development resources for those serving the field of PreK–12 education. By providing practical, hands-on materials, Corwin continues to carry out the promise of its motto: **"Helping Educators Do Their Work Better."**